END TO END

END TO END

JOHN O'GROATS, BROKEN SPOKES AND A DOG CALLED GRETNA

ALISTAIR MCGUINNESS

Half a World Away

Contents

1.	The Middle	1
2.	The Beginning	3
3.	The End-to-enders	5
4.	Changes	9
5.	The Passenger	13
6.	Wherever I Lay my Hat (That's my Home)	23
7.	Day 1: Once in a Lifetime	27
8.	Day 2: Road to Hell	33
9.	Day 3: I Don't Like Mondays	43
10.	Day 4: Breathe	49
11.	Day 5: Road to Nowhere	59
12.	Day 6: Day Tripper	65
13.	Day 7: He Ain't Heavy, He's My Brother	77
14.	Day 8: Sunshine after the Rain	83
15.	Day 9: Tequila Sunrise	99
16.	Day 10: Riders on the Storm	109
17.	Day 11: Three miles high	115
18.	Day 12: Don't Pay the Ferryman	119
19.	Day 13: Champagne Supernova	127
20.	John O'Groats	139
21.	Gretna	141
22.	Later	143
23.	Authors Note	145
24.	Acknowledgments	147

1

The Middle

I never noticed the first cloud, or the second, but the third was hard to ignore. Just how they had eluded us was something of a mystery. I stopped pedalling, and for the first time in an hour, looked up from the road to study the sky.

The hazy blue that we had cycled beneath all morning was being displaced by a band of pale clouds sweeping down from the north. With each mile that we travelled, they gathered strength and loomed ominously on the horizon, turning dark and moody as the border approached.

By mid-afternoon, they were closing in on all sides, akin to the pincer movement of attacking Zulus. The black clouds resembled the head and horns of a mighty bull, and we were heading straight into their midst. Cars refused to slow and hurtled close by, just as the first bolt of lightning pierced the sky.

I dropped to the rear of the pack, stared through the gloom at Nick's luminous yellow poncho, and wiped raindrops from my face. Alan was out there somewhere too, his khaki poncho rendering him invisible against the English countryside. Cocooned inside my poncho, I concentrated solely on keeping the handlebars straight, as articulated lorries roared alongside. We were halfway between Land's End and John O'Groats, and within two hours, one of our lives would be changed forever.

2

The Beginning

The sun was low, casting welcome shadows across the country lane as it dropped behind the treetops, adding a touch of warmth to the thin trail of clouds lingering in the evening sky. Three men crested the rise, riding bicycles in single file, their eyes scanning the buildings in search of a place to rest. Their flushed faces broke into wide smiles as they read the welcoming sign and coasted through a gabled entrance into a large courtyard, where they came to a stop in breathless silence.

The first rider to dismount was Nick, and he wore Lycra shorts, a polo T-shirt, and a baseball cap turned backwards. He removed his cap and wraparound sunglasses, stood on tiptoe, and dropped to his knees. He then rolled onto his back, splayed his long legs wide across the floor, and whispered hoarsely, 'This place better have hot showers and comfy beds, Alistair.'

I was the second rider to dismount and the one named Alistair. I was too exhausted to answer and sought refuge on a wooden bench situated by the doorway, where I quietly drained the remaining water in my bottle. While sipping the contents, the muscles in my legs stiffened rapidly, causing an involuntary spasm as cramp gripped my lower calf and I winced in pain. I dropped onto the floor, gripped my leg, and with trembling forearms, attempted to stretch the locked muscle.

The third rider to dismount was the tallest of the three. He removed his baseball cap, revealing a crop of bleached hair, and chuckled softly at the sorrowful sight before him. At twenty-eight years of age, Alan stepped past his friends, and for the first time in his life, entered a youth hostel.

It was day two of our Land's End to John O'Groats bike ride, and in our quest to become end-to-enders, we had just cycled 89 miles during one of the hottest days of the year.

4 End to End

3

The End-to-enders

"Begin with the end in mind."
— Stephen Covey

Becoming an end-to-ender requires the traveller to journey from the most westerly point of England (Land's End) to the northwestern tip of Scotland (John O'Groats). Although the signposts at either end state the total distance as 874 miles, the infinite choice of roads, tracks and footpaths make the actual amount a unique figure for each end-to-ender, with many clocking over 1,000 miles.

You can complete the challenge in any direction, and there are many theories about which is the most efficient (think wind direction). However, we chose bottom to top, quite simply because Land's End was nearer to our home.

Purists will note that John O'Groats is not the most northern part of Scotland. This accolade belongs to a wild expanse of spectacular cliffs known as Dunnet Head, located eleven miles northwest of John O'Groats. For the view alone, and if you have the energy, time and motivation to do so, it is worth the additional journey.

For those that have undertaken the end-to-end adventure, modes of transport have ranged from the traditional to the obscure. Since the first documented walk by brothers John and Robert Naylor in 1871, thousands of people have undertaken the epic challenge.

There is rarely a summer that goes by without somebody making a claim to be the fastest, oldest, or youngest end-to-ender. As I write this story in 2016, the oldest known person to undertake the adventure is Tony Rathbone, who completed the challenge aged 81 years and 16 days.

The wackiest attempt to date must belong to Sean Conway, who decided to follow up his 2008 bike ride with the first ever swim from Land's End to John O'Groats. By the time he dragged himself from the North Sea and staggered to the finish line, 135 days had passed. Dressed in a full-length Speedo swimsuit and iron-grey swim hat, the only part of his body on display was his weathered face. This was partly hidden by a frizzy ginger beard, grown specifically to protect against jellyfish stings.

In 2015, he ran from John O'Groats to Land's End in six weeks. This epic feat was the equivalent of completing 38 continual marathons, and in doing so, he became the first person to complete the ultimate British triathlon. His story is eccentricity and adventurism at its best and proves once again that we can achieve so much if we have the desire and strength to do so.

Apart from those attempting record times, the vast majority of end-to-enders are thrilled to finish the journey unscathed. Some will undertake the challenge for charity; others will complete it for a sense of achievement. Everyone has their reasons and are in every way unique.

Imagine, if you will, that on any one day (mainly in spring and summer) there will be hundreds of people travelling from one extremity to the other. Most will be on bikes, in cars or walking. A few brave souls will attempt to run the full distance, and even Penny Farthings have been sighted at John O'Groats. As far as I know, space hoppers, scooters and pogo sticks have never been used. Yet.

All in all, that's a lot of people at any one time, going up or coming down, passing each other, oblivious to each other, and from time to time (normally near the beginning and end), meeting and congratulating each other.

I hadn't grown up wishing to be an end-to-ender. But it's an adventure that occurred 20 years ago with two friends, Alan and Nick. Along the way, we discovered the joys of friendship, enjoyed British beer, embraced the open road, appreciated the importance of spare spokes, stayed in our first (and only) youth hostel, and met many quirky individuals. For one of us, the bike ride was a game changer. For them, life would never be the same after reaching Scotland.

So why tell the story some two decades later? That's a good question, but the reason is simple: we've recently decided to do it all over again. To mark the 20th anniversary of becoming end-to-enders, we will once again cycle from Land's End to John O'Groats. Only this time, we plan to book ahead!

I now live in Australia, and once I had made the decision and booked my return ticket, I decided to hunt down my travel journal from the summer of 1996. As I read about our exploits, the joyful memories flooded back. In this book, I will share them with you in the hope they will inspire. Young, old, fit or not, it is never too late to consider a new adventure.

4

Changes

"If you come to a fork in the road, take it."
— **Yogi Berra**

Brothers have their uses. Take my oldest brother, Dave, for example. He is dependable, logical, knowledgeable and hard working. More importantly, in 1996 he had a bike, which was something I was in urgent need of at the time. At 30 years of age, I was lodging with Dave and should have been capable of affording my own bike. But for six years I had struggled with our mum's death, after her long illness with cancer. This emotional event subsequently sent me into a spiral of failed relationships, missed mortgage payments, and lager-induced weekends. For many years after her death, I was in a constant state of change, eager to please others, but restless with myself.

I worked feverishly to fuel an appetite for adventure travel, but was too afraid to leave my day job. I spent three weeks per year on overseas trips, resulting in a smorgasbord of mini-adventures, including camping in the African wilderness, boating along the Mekong Delta, and learning to ice-climb in the Alps. Weekends would alternate between three extremes: working overtime, nightclubbing and hill-walking.

I survived on my sister's home-cooked dinners. I was also infatuated with the idea of moving to another country, which meant that relationships rarely lasted more than three or four months. After another abrupt ending, due to an argument over the distance and isolation of living in New Zealand, I found myself alone once more.

Within 24 hours, I was on a stag weekend in the seaside town of Blackpool, sharing a late night kebab with a close friend, Alan. He is one of those characters that attract more friends than he knows what to do with. He is tall, broad shouldered, with a cheeky grin, cropped hair, and a bright round face. The life and soul of the party would be a fitting description, and back then, when out on the town, he rarely seemed to be without a beer and an audience.

Stag weekends can turn messy, but not this one. Jason was the groom-to-be and was under strict instructions from his fiancé to return home without making it to the front page of the Blackpool Gazette. That left Alan and I without a mission, and with Jason safely back in his hotel, the thought of cavorting with late night revellers, although appealing, was overtaken by the lure of a late night kebab!

It was after midnight when we slouched on a windswept bench, overlooking the oily waters of the Irish Sea, and chomped on the greasy fast food. Between bites, we chuckled about the evenings' antics and once again contemplated revisiting the 80s nightclub to search for remnants of the stag party.

Just before we returned to the Golden Mile, Alan asked, 'Well, Ali, any more adventures planned for this year?

I was quiet for a second, then answered, 'To be truthful, I'm in need of a change. It's been six years since my mum died, and I think it's time for me to grow up.'

He picked the remains of his kebab from the wrapper and replied, 'Did you know my mum is sick? She has cancer.'

There was a moment of silence between us, broken by the faint roll of waves breaking gently on the beach, somewhere in the darkness. Before I could muster a worthy reply, he changed the subject and asked, 'Did you also hear that I'm cycling from Land's End to John O'Groats with Nick Hart?'

I knew who Nick was and felt a flicker of jealousy. At work, he was a popular man, slightly eccentric and prone to the odd mishap. This trait, together with wearing glasses, had earned him the nickname of Mr. Magoo, after the shortsighted cartoon character. Whether this offended him or not, nobody really knew. He was such a carefree character that nothing seemed to faze him.

My mind whirred with suitable answers — to wish them good luck and how amazing that would be, but as I went to reply, the only words that came out were, 'Can I come too?' Then came a moment of clarity as I whispered, 'We could raise money for cancer during the bike ride.'

Alan took a moment to reply, then answered quietly, 'Sounds like a plan. I guess Nick won't mind, but I'd better ask him, just to make sure.'

I punched him playfully on the shoulder and replied, 'Look, I don't want to force myself into the ride. If Nick wants it to be just you two, then I can live with that.'

As we stood to leave, I noticed a tremble in Alan's voice as he tossed the wrapper in a nearby bin and said, 'Cancer is such a bastard, Ali.'

With that, we set off in search of the stag party.

Soon to be married Jason headed home by minibus the next morning, still unscathed. But eager to stretch the weekend to the maximum, Alan and I convinced two friends to abandon their ride home and join us for a Sunday pub-crawl of Blackpool's sea front. At sunset we abandoned the tourist traps and chanced our luck in a backstreet bar, away from the flashing lights and bingo halls.

The difference was sobering, and we were soon playing pool with hustlers, homeless, and harlots. Not that they were threatening, despite their dark attire and guttural language. By nightfall, Alan was arm-wrestling a pony-tailed biker, Peter was swapping phone numbers with a Jamaican backpacker, and Scott was asleep by the jukebox. It was time to get out of town.

The only transport available was a passing taxi, and four hours later, we paid a hefty sum to the red-eyed driver who had silently driven us hundreds of miles south. As I fumbled with the key to my brother's front door, Alan woke in the back seat, stuck his head out of the cab window and yelled, 'Nick just texted me and the answer is yes. He also says to let you know that he doesn't do youth hostels. By the way, we leave in six weeks.'

Undrawn curtains forced an abrupt end to my morning lie in, as shards of summer sun streaked through the bedroom window. Luckily, an afternoon start at the car factory offered a few hours' respite, so I made my way downstairs in search of tea and toast. Just as the kettle boiled, the late night conversation with Alan flooded back —finding out that his mum had cancer, asking to join the ride, talking about raising money for charity.

I also remembered hailing a taxi for a four-hour journey home. More wasted money, when I needed now to buy a bike. But there was another way; I knew just where to find one.

Dave was working out of town, either programming robots in European car factories or trekking across the Lake District. I was unsure which. While he was away, my tasks were to mow the lawn and pay the bills. But the lawn could wait another day and there were no red letters on the hallway floor, which meant I had a few hours to spare until work commenced, and I was eager to check out his bike.

I made tea, found the garage key, and stepped inside. A waft of stagnant air caught at the back of my throat as I fumbled with the light switch and searched for the bike among toolboxes, ladders, shelving, and gardening utensils.

The bike was hidden under a dusty tarpaulin, and as I ripped the cover away, my heart raced in anticipation. It fell to the floor, and I reached out and touched the spokes, running my fingers across each gnarled tyre. It looked to be in pristine condition, but as I lifted it from the floor, it became apparent that it was designed for comfort, not speed. It wasn't all bad news. The racing-green colour scheme gave it a classical look, and the wide handlebars were decorated with a chrome bell that rang with a crisp sound as I pinged the lever.

With a soft gel saddle, ultra-long mudguards and ten gears to choose from, it was perfect for cycling to the shops, or to country pubs on warm summer's evenings.

But if men on Penny Farthings could complete the end-to-end journey, then so could I. Even on Dave's bike. Right there and then I convinced myself that he would be happy for me to take it for a spin. All I needed to do now was get fit.

5

The Passenger

"Every time I see an adult on a bicycle, I no longer despair for the future of the human race."
— **H. G. Wells**

Nick lives with his charming wife, Karen, in a delightful country town called Ampthill in the county of Bedfordshire, and it's here that we met to make our plan. The side of their home was festooned with hanging baskets, filled with an array of wildflowers in full bloom. Their front door was already ajar, and as we approached, Karen appeared and welcomed us both with open arms.

'Anyone for tea?' she announced cheerfully. 'Or is that a silly question?'

Nick answered for her as he bounded into the hallway, holding aloft two bottles of beer and ushering us into his garage, teeming with remnants of his sporting pastimes. Boat parts were scattered on a workbench, and water skis were propped against a wall. Everywhere I looked there was an assortment of bike frames, wheels and gears.

'What are you searching for?' I asked as he rummaged through a tea chest.

'I'm after a map to help plan our trip. But I want to go a different way this time.'

'I didn't know you'd cycled it already.'

'There's a lot you don't know about me,' he replied casually and continued to search for his map. It was true. I worked in the same factory, but there were 15,000 other employees under the same roof. I often bumped into him, but he was usually absorbed in maintenance tasks that involved oil, grease, bearings, or robot parts. I rarely spoke with him in detail. Not like this.

I had heard he was far sportier than his Magoo tag, and now that I was inside his social circle, I could see that this was true. It felt good to be a part of the forthcoming adventure, and I found myself smiling as I looked around the garage. While Nick muttered to himself and tore open boxes, I searched for Alan. He was in the corner, studying a collection of Shimano gears.

My daydream was broken when Nick stood up and announced, 'Ah, here it is.' In his hand he was holding an A4-sized book. The front cover was emblazoned with the words, *AA Road Map of Britain, 1975*. 'This will do nicely,' he declared with pride.

'Do for what?' Alan asked as he replaced the gears and studied the faded front cover.

'For our route.'

'But that's an old map. The M25 wasn't even constructed in 1975,' I informed him.

He smiled and replied, 'That's OK because we won't be on the M25 during our bike ride.'

'We will if you're map reading,' Alan retorted with a chuckle.

'I've got an up-to-date map of youth hostels in my rucksack, if that will help,' I chirped.

Nick removed his glasses and from across the garage gave me the thousand-yard stare. 'Ali, I don't *do* youth hostels. After I've been cycling all day, I want a decent room with a comfortable bed, and in the morning, I want a full English breakfast, with eggs, bacon and mushrooms. I don't want organic muesli served by a bearded university drop-out wearing a Ban the Bomb T-shirt.' Before I had time to reply, he continued. 'In Wales, I want grilled lamb for breakfast, and in Scotland, I would like to be served haggis and black pudding by grey-haired farmers' wives.'

As he paused for breath, I blurted out, 'Nick, I think you have the wrong idea about youth hostels. Compulsory dormitories, cold showers and organic muesli are just myths. I reckon we'll have a blast. You know, the feeling of meeting travellers from across the world and engaging in stimulating conversation while preparing noodles in the cosmopolitan kitchen.'

He put his hands to his ears and cried out, 'Please stop. You're making it sound even worse.'

'Well, we don't have to cook dinner with anyone, but YHAs have moved on. In fact, you might be pleasantly surprised.' I turned to Alan and asked, 'What do you think?'

He took a swig of beer, grinned and said, 'Well, you know me. I'll try anything once.'

We reconvened in the dining room, and while Karen supplied copious amounts of pizza, washed down with a selection of

Bedfordshire ales, we dismembered the map, tearing out page after page and then spreading them across the carpet.

It soon resembled a rectangle mosaic, with southwest at the bottom, northeast at the top and the midlands in between. Here before us were the arteries of Britain. Blue lines, wider than any other strokes on the map, depicted motorways. Since motorways were designed and constructed in the late 1950s, they have become an integral part of Britain's traffic infrastructure, and bicycles are banned on them for very good reasons.

But we weren't after the quickest route. Ideally, we wanted a mixture of direct roads to ensure we cycled in the right direction, and quieter back roads to add a sense of calm and escape from traffic.

Main roads, depicted in red on our map, are designed to link major towns as directly as possible, which means long, straight stretches. Many have strategically placed dual carriageways (on inclines), designed to allow vehicles to overtake slow movers such as caravans and articulated lorries.

We didn't envisage overtaking any traffic, apart from maybe space hoppers, and so we knelt down to observe the thin, squiggly green lines. These were minor roads. Our hope was that they would wind sedately through rolling farmland, past hedgerows and woodland, and alongside small rivers and gurgling streams.

Many of these country roads act as conduits between villages, and some circumnavigate industrial towns. This means that Sunday drivers, stressed commuters looking for alternative routes, boy racers in fast cars, and cycle clubs also use them.

Nick took out a fluorescent green marker, highlighted Land's End, and then declared, 'Well, guys, where to next?'

I was keen to visit specific places, for personal reasons, and asked, 'How about Newquay for our first night? Steve lives there, and I'd imagine the weekends are quite lively in summer.' Steve Eagles was a close friend and known by us all. He had once worked alongside us at the car factory, but escaped a year earlier to become an adventure sports instructor.

Alan nodded in acceptance, and Nick responded by smudging Newquay in green ink.

'OK, where to after that?' he asked.

He had previously calculated that each day's travel would require approximately 70 miles of cycling. Land's End to Newquay was about 43 miles, and simple arithmetic meant we had to cycle further the following day to make up. For a few seconds, we pondered the map of

Cornwall with its intricate selection of green squiggly lines, hugging the fractured shoreline and meaning dramatic views of the ocean. One road dominated the map, leading directly through the heart of Cornwall, past the bleak expanse of Bodmin Moor towards Exeter in Devon.

Without the need for consultation, he ran the marker from Newquay along the A30 towards Exeter, then tapped my shoulder and said, 'Well, you wanted to stay in a youth hostel, and we might as well get it over and done with early. Just make sure you book us into a family room, not a dormitory filled with international students on their first gap year!'

I smiled in agreement and made a mental note to book us into a hostel in Exeter. There were a few must see places that made it onto our map, including a visit to Wales (so that we could cycle through three countries), Gretna Green in Scotland (first village in Scotland), Chester (friends to visit), Liverpool (The Beatles) and Shap Hill in the Lake District (an incline not to be missed, according to Nick). Edinburgh also sounded appealing, and so did the Scottish Highlands, where my Dad loved to roam and often got lost in the mist.

With only two weeks' holiday available to complete the trip, it was imperative that we stuck to direct roads as often as possible, but we all agreed that it was not a strict plan. After all, it was the journey together that mattered, not just the final destination.

With the map stapled together, Nick returned to his garage and appeared with a black canvas bag, coated in a fine layer of mildew. 'There you go, Ali. These were the panniers I used on my first end-to-end, many years ago. You can borrow them if you like.'

I was extremely grateful and took hold of the heavy fabric. I could feel something inside rattling around as I placed it on the floor. I peeled open the main compartment, peered inside and plucked out the dried remnants of a discarded apple core and a squashed Mars Bar. The words on the wrapper said, 'Enjoy before October 1982.'

In the hallway, Karen appeared, to send us off with more hugs and kisses. 'I will see you in Scotland, lads,' she explained eagerly and then said, 'When you're at work next, can you please give a spare set of clothes to Nick, so that Sam and I can take them to the Scottish border for you? That way you only have to carry clothes for the first week.'

I wasn't aware that Karen was going to meet us halfway, so asked, 'Who's Sam? Are you both tagging along during the second week?'

She smiled and replied, 'Sam is my good friend. We're going to have a girlie week in Scotland while you boys do your cycle thing. We might bump into you a few times, and we'll drive you home from John O'Groats.'

She touched Nick's shoulder and explained, 'He loves finding husbands for Sam, don't you?'

Nick laughed and replied, 'Just the one so far.' And then explained how he had set Sam up with his friend, which swiftly led to romance and marriage. But that had been many years before. The marriage was now over, and Sam had been single and happy for a long time.

'What's she like?' I asked. Karen beamed proudly and replied, 'She's lovely, of course. That's why she's my friend! You'll both meet her soon enough, and besides, it will give you something to think about during those long rides across the lonely moors. But just so you know, she adores live music and is partial to a glass of wine.'

Having a lift home was something I hadn't yet considered, so it was a relief to have this part of the equation already organised. As for spare clothes being hand-delivered to Scotland, I couldn't have wished for more. Meeting Karen and Sam at the halfway point was beginning to sound like a good idea, and with the grateful knowledge that I would have fresh underpants in Scotland, I bade them farewell and set off home with Alan.

On the journey back, he challenged me to ride the 12-mile trip in under an hour and set off at speed along the country lanes. Initially, I felt euphoric at how well the evening had gone. I was going on an adventure and even had a pair of panniers to use. Alan's pace was relentless, and he charged up the first major incline, leaving me far behind. When I eventually reached the top, a stab of pain caused me to pull over sharply as pizza and beer grumbled in my stomach.

'Must have been those jalapenos,' I said while catching my breath. Alan gave me a puzzled look, although I sensed what he was thinking. How could I struggle after such a short ride? I shrugged away the burning sensation in my chest and climbed back onto the saddle, desperate to mask the nervousness that I felt about holding them back.

Nick had calculated our total distance would be close to 900 miles. The plan was to complete the ride in thirteen days flat. If we kept to schedule, we would commence on a Saturday and arrive at our destination on a Thursday. Then we would drive to Inverness on the Friday to celebrate and return home on the Saturday. It seemed like an arduous task, and during the final miles' home, my mind raced with self-doubt.

They were competent riders, naturally fit, with decent bikes. Maybe Nick would be able to build me a bike from all those spare parts in his garage, I wondered. During the remainder of the ride, I contemplated asking him. But I'd already forced myself onto the trip and didn't want to compromise my newfound friendship by asking for any more gifts. The bike was more than capable. I just needed to get fitter!

There is a sense of invincibility during your 20s that basically says, I can get away with anything that I want to achieve without much training. Some call it ignorance. Others call it youth. But I was no longer a youngster. I was nearly 31 years of age and stood five feet eight inches on a good day. Yes, I played in a football team most weekends and had once run a 10km race in under 38 minutes, but that had been a decade earlier and was before I had broken my leg in a nightclub dance routine!

For over a decade, a combination of shift work, sporting injuries and bad habits had taken their toll. But mental strength had pulled me through before, and it was this trait, plus an 'Above Average' level of fitness marked on my gym scorecard, that I was planning to rely on. Alan lived nearby (I had also lodged with him), and over the following weeks, we found time to cycle through the surrounding countryside in an attempt to get fit.

In truth, our training schedule became excuses for cycling from one village pub to another. During one such ride (after a day at work repairing broken robots) we headed into the local countryside to trail blaze along ancient footpaths and winding roads.

Evening hikers, dressed in shorts and carrying daypacks, waved as we passed by, and more than once, we caught sight of Muntjac deer grazing alongside the tree line. These small, stocky animals are native to South Asia, but some managed to escape from Woburn Abbey Wildlife Park in the early 20th Century and their descendants are now widespread throughout England and Wales.

It was hard to imagine that we were only a few miles from the drab shopping mall and tired high street with which Luton Town is synonymous, and I felt sad to think that very few visitors to the nearby airport would ever take the time to experience the surrounding area. For many people, Luton is a gateway to faraway sunshine via budget airlines and not a location for exploring. Yet here we were, in sight of the control tower, cycling through rolling farmland and along narrow roads shrouded by ancient woodlands. Every few miles, we encountered charming villages, sprinkled with thatched cottages, duck ponds, and welcoming pubs.

After two hours of hard riding, I was thankful for the setting sun, and without a word, we turned towards town and cycled under the flight path as 737s began their noisy descent towards the airport. The White Horse public house in the village of Tea Green was a welcome sight, and we entered the bar with a sweaty saunter, proud of our concerted efforts on such a fine summer's evening.

The pub car park was filled with cars, as visiting townsfolk embraced the humid weather. While walking through the open door, I immediately appreciated the landlord's choice of music and found myself humming along to *Echo Beach* as we headed towards the bar.

Alan studied the ales on tap, picked a seasonal brew, and ordered two pints. While the beers were being poured, I settled onto a bar stool and reminisced about the last few weeks. With each ride I was getting fitter, but time was fast running out. Alan had nothing to worry about. He was relatively young (under thirty), naturally athletic, and he had a worthy bike. But I didn't feel fazed by Alan's strengths. It gave me hope. And I knew that he and Nick would look after me during the journey.

The ales arrived, and as he passed mine over, he said, 'Here you go, mate. Well done on tonight.' We clinked glasses and chatted for a few minutes, before I went in search of the toilet.

On my return, he was in deep discussion with the barman, and as I sat back onto my stool, the barman pointed out a framed certificate on the adjacent wall that declared, in scrolled words, he was an end-to-ender. I could sense he wanted to talk about his exploits, but a steady stream of customers continually pulled him away. During our second beer, the crowd thinned and the cool evening air persuaded those outside to either head home or take refuge in the pub. The barman introduced himself as the landlord, then leaned towards us and asked softly, 'So, when do you lads plan to ride?'

'Oh, in about two weeks,' Alan replied.

He nodded knowingly. 'Great stuff. So how's your training going?'

Alan answered, 'Oh not too bad. This was our longest training ride so far. We cycled for over two hours this evening, didn't we, Ali?'

I nodded in agreement and sipped the summer ale, while *Echo Beach* resonated once more in the background.

'How many months have you been in training?' he enquired.

'We only decided to ride a short while ago. So we've been kind of training for about four weeks in all,' he chortled.

The landlord made a stifled sound and in a direct tone said, 'You are joking, of course.'

'No,' we managed to say in unison, and Alan continued by explaining our simple tactics. 'We'll be all right. You know how it goes — cycle hard during the day, a few beers at night. Then get a good night's sleep, followed by a hearty breakfast, and repeat for twelve more days.'

The landlord's eyes were wider now as he asked, 'What type of bikes do you have?' Alan pointed towards the pub garden and said, 'You can see if you want.'

He followed us outside to investigate and smiled appreciably at Alan's bright yellow bike. It was sleek, and more importantly, it had the technical components to merit such a ride, with Shimano gears, slick tyres and new brakes.

'Well this looks like it will make it. Just.' He lifted the bike off the ground with three fingers, stared at Alan and said, 'In my opinion, the frame is a few seasons too old, but you look fit enough to get away with it.'

He never bothered lifting up my bike. Instead, he asked, 'Is this your training bike, mate?' I grinned widely and declared, 'No it's my brother's, but he's in Canada at the moment, and I thought it could do with a run to John O'Groats. Do you like it?' Before he could reply, I continued my flurry, 'I've decided to call it the Donegal Flyer, in memory of my Mum.'

He looked over at Alan, then back at me and said. 'Sounds like a fitting name. Was your mother a pilot?'

'No, but she was from Donegal.'

'Well, you'll need the luck of the Irish to get there on that thing, mate.' In an instant, his eyes turned serious and he asked in a fatherly way, 'How many weeks' holiday are you planning to take to get there? Three, I hope.'

I chuckled nervously, looked at Alan and said, 'No, the same as him. Just two weeks.'

He looked down at my footwear and said, 'Do you have cycling shoes?'

'Yes, of course, I'm wearing them now.'

'No mate, they're trainers — for running after buses and kicking balls. I mean proper bike shoes, with cleats that click into clipless pedals. They're the future, you know?'

'No, all I have is these trainers. I got them from the Arndale last week.'

'What about cycling shorts?'

'I've got a pair of football shorts.'

'Panniers?'

'Yes! I've borrowed a second-hand set from Nick. He's our third rider and the project leader.'

'Where's he then?' the landlord asked, looking towards the village green.

'At home, probably eating pizza and guzzling home-brewed beer,' Alan replied quickly.

'Are you guys taking the piss?' Before we could answer, he asked one more question. 'Can you repair broken spokes?'

'The Donegal Flyer won't let me down,' I assured him.

'Well, guys, your lack of preparation is evident, but you seem determined enough to get to the end. Come inside and have a free pint on me. You'll be burning a lot of carbs on the way, and it's the least I can do.'

6

Wherever I Lay my Hat (That's my Home)

"I am just going outside and may be some time."
— **Lawrence "Titus" Oates**

During the week leading up to the ride, I replaced the chunky tyres with the slickest ones possible, then lubricated the chain and fiddled with the gear sprockets. The Donegal Flyer hummed sweetly, and as a final touch, I attached a speedometer to the handlebars.

On Thursday night, Alan and I headed into town with friends for a celebratory send off. The nightclub DJ announced our planned adventure over the microphone, then presented us with a bottle of champagne, and we danced until closing time.

An early start for work on Friday morning took the edge of our premature celebrations, and eight hours later, we clocked off for two weeks' holiday. The car was filled with luggage, water bottles, crisps and other essentials, and the bikes were securely strapped above the boot, blocking all views from the rear window. My brother, Matthew, volunteered to drive us to Land's End, and we estimated that the trip from Bedfordshire would take about five hours.

While we headed towards the motorway, Alan handpicked a selection of summer tunes, and with windows down, the sounds of the Manic Street Preachers and Oasis filled the air. In the distance, blue sky broke through a thin band of pale clouds as we joined thousands of others who had followed the advice of the weatherman.

As we travelled south and west, the houses and industrial units dwindled, replaced by sun-drenched fields that dipped and rose alongside the motorway. Freshly cut hay adorned many paddocks, their barrels rolled into small groups of four or five. It reminded me that another summer was nearing its end. How had it passed so quickly?

I knew deep down that I needed to prepare. Not for the bike ride. I had done some training, although nowhere near enough. But I had to start planning for the rest of my life; maybe the ride would renew my confidence. Far in the distance, a series of small hills dominated the horizon, their shallow summits dotted with majestic oak trees. They had grown from seeds over many decades and were now in full bloom. I needed to make plans for the future, so that I had something to show for my life in 10 or 20 years. Maybe this bike ride would be the first seed planted.

Matthew pulled me back to reality, calling my name out loud to check our whereabouts on the map. We had left the motorway and were now on long, straight stretches of bitumen. Sometimes we drove up long stretches of hills, and very soon after, hurtled down the other side. The angles were not severe, but for heavy vehicles and those pulling trailers or caravans, the effects were significant. Slow moving caravans created a backlog of vehicles in their wake, all searching for a gap in the oncoming traffic or a passing lane. Warning signs displayed the distance to the next dual carriageway, and cars tail-gated each other in anticipation.

Matthew found himself stuck behind a rickety caravan, just as a dual carriageway sign appeared. A blaze of lights in our wing mirrors signalled the arrival of a black BMW, looming close to our bike rack as it sought to overtake when possible. Just as the road split into two, Matthew veered into the overtaking lane and floored the accelerator, but in reality, not a lot happened. The speed of our vehicle remained exactly the same despite the additional revs. Four men, three panniers filled with clothes, one overnight bag, three bikes, and one high mileage Vauxhall Astra meant only one thing — we couldn't overtake the caravan. In fact, the caravan decided to speed up. For fifteen miles it had crawled at 65mph, and the moment we had a chance to overtake, the caravan owner decided to show us what he really had.

The angle of incline began to change. Not by much, but just enough to slow the caravan, and within half a mile, we were alongside the car that was pulling it. It was hard to forget the BMW behind us, as he was now so close to the bike rack that we could clearly see the driver's eyes staring wildly ahead.

Matthew drew past the caravan, and we got our first look at the owner. He had a wild thatch of grey hair, far more on his head than the hair of the occupants in our car put together, and his eyes were hidden behind a pair of Roy Orbison glasses.

A sticker in the rear window of his four-wheel drive vehicle declared a love of Captain Morgan's Rum, and as we inched past, I sneaked a peek at his partner. She was fast asleep in the passenger seat, open mouthed and oblivious to his quest for glory as their caravan snaked along the main road.

Up ahead, the warning sign for a single lane came into view, and I called out, 'Pull in, Matt, we won't make it.'

Matthew was no longer with us. It was a duel to the end. With foot to the floor and the dulcet tones of Noel Gallagher pulsating from the speakers, we edged past the car just as the dual carriage returned to a single road. In the side mirrors, I distinctly noticed the bonnet of the BMW dip sharply, followed by a puff of burnt rubber as the driver braked sharply then pulled in behind the caravan.

The single road ahead was gloriously devoid of traffic, but fast flowing in the opposite direction, and as we passed the four-wheel drive with the caravan, it returned to its legal speed and dropped far behind. We never saw it, or the BMW, again.

By sunset, the music playlist had stopped, and so had we. Both lanes were blocked with traffic, and we settled into a stop-go, stop-go existence, trying to ignore the smell of burnt diesel permeating through the car's air conditioning system.

'What's Torquay like at this time of year?' Nick asked as a signpost crept into view.

'Well, it must be better than a traffic jam,' Alan declared.

We took the detour, and within an hour, drove past a signpost that read *Welcome to the English Riviera.*

Rows of tall palm trees lined the manicured streets, giving an air of grandeur and a sense of credibility to the Riviera claim. We easily located the coastal strip, where streets filled with grand old houses had been restored or renovated to cater for the summer influx of visitors. Small, family-run bed and breakfast establishments sat side-by-side larger buildings with names such as The Riviera Hotel, Ocean View Motel and The Riviera Retreat. Most establishments we passed had neon signs in the front window, all illuminated in red, informing us that there were "No Vacancies."

Other guesthouses displayed large boards on their front lawns, decorated with their name. Underneath, attached by chains, they would add one of two wooden signs. One board would read *No Vacancy*. The other, in theory, read *Vacancy*. I guessed that the vacancy signs were most popular on Monday mornings and could envisage the scene each week as proprietors stood in their front gardens, swapping their signs, and peeking along the street to see how many other places were now empty. But now it was a Friday evening, and the only signs swinging in the breeze were the ones that read *No Vacancy*.

We drove alongside one row of guesthouses, then another, and after multiple sorties, came to the conclusion that Torquay was full for the night. As we contemplated returning to the main road, Matthew noticed a hotel without a wooden or neon sign, and within minutes, we were all standing outside the front door.

The owner was slightly plump, with bright blue eyes and mousey hair that rested on her shoulders. She wore a kitchen apron over a floral blouse and tentatively opened the door to eye the potential guests. Before we opened our mouths to ask for a room, she explained quickly, 'The chain that supports the *Vacancy* sign snapped off this evening, and I do have two rooms available. But I'm awfully sorry — I don't normally allow all-male parties.'

There was a brief silence as we stood to attention on the doorstep, trying our best to look like decent, law-abiding citizens. Then she explained, 'You know, with all the noise and mess you men tend to make…'

Nick cleared his throat, removed his cap and spoke on our behalf, 'Well, today is your lucky day. Matthew here is our coach and doesn't stay up late, or drink beer. We three are on our way to Cornwall, to cycle from Land's End to John O'Groats and in the morning will be up with the lark.'

She smiled softly, eyed us warily and said, 'OK, on first impressions you seem like a friendly bunch. But please, no noise after ten, and if you behave yourselves, I'll cook you a delicious breakfast in the morning.'

We were true to our word and so was she. The night started off with an amble along the bracing sea-front, followed by a few beers, a curry, and a visit to the Riviera Nightclub. It was after midnight when we quietly tiptoed along the corridor to our rooms.

I couldn't help feeling, as we turned out the lights, that we were in a bubble. Nightclubs and cycling didn't mix. While lying in bed, I thought back to the boisterous karaoke session at a riverfront pub and the holiday girls that joined us for a rendition of Elvis songs and the encore of Queen's *Bicycle Song*.

I don't think anyone we met during the evening cared or believed that we were eleven hours away from commencing a thirteen-day bike ride. In the throng of sweat, flashing lights, disco music and 80s flashbacks, we were just three men, slightly drunk, talking nonsense, and dancing erratically. With this thought, I smiled and closed my eyes. It was going to be an interesting journey.

7

Day 1: Once in a Lifetime

"You can't stop the waves, but you can learn to surf."
— Jon Kabat-Zinn

Land's End to Newquay (45 miles)

An early departure was required to ensure that we didn't start the bike ride too late, so it was with a sense of purpose that we devoured the cooked breakfast, thanked the patron, and continued our journey.

Land's End is a place of extraordinary beauty, where visitors embrace the experience of standing on a remote cliff-top at the westernmost point in England. It's also a privately run enterprise, with cafés, a pub, boutique shops, and a post office. As I write this in 2016, I note that there are many more man-made (family) attractions today than twenty years earlier.

Our official enrollment took place at the post office, where we signed a logbook in the presence of the postmaster, a genial man by the name of Ron. Despite the small queue of tourists waiting to purchase postcards, he gave us plenty of his time and cheerfully explained the process of recording each end-to-ender. He also informed us that completed books are stored at the post office as official records.

Once we had made it to John O'Groats, all we needed to do was sign the logbook at the main hotel and a certificate would be posted to our homes. With our names now inscribed, we thanked Ron and made our way past a collection of gift shops towards the Land's End signpost.

Perched close to the cliff-top, the signpost was sectioned off by a chain link fence, and a small fee was required to stand alongside the iconic sign for an official photo. Markers displayed the distance in miles to four locations: New York (3147); Isles of Scilly (28); Longships Lighthouse (1.5); and John O'Groats (874). Visitors could also add their hometown to a "spare" pointer, and the distance would be calculated and displayed on the signpost alongside the permanent locations.

With the photo taken, we pushed our bikes to the cliff edge to gaze over the water. 200 feet below, feisty waves broke onto granite boulders, fractured long ago from the cliff edge. The water to our left was the English Channel, and close to shore, a flotilla of sailing boats raced around a series of buoys. Further out, fishing trawlers carved though the water, leaving trails of white water in their wake as they headed home with their catch of the day.

I gazed at the wide stretch of water to our right, where cargo ships sat low on the horizon. This was the mighty Atlantic, with no landfall between Land's End and the USA. Apart from the wind, tugging at a raised St. George flag, the only other sound was a lone gull skimming along the cliff tops, its shrill squawk drowned out by a young family shouting ice-cream orders to their mother.

As we stood on the plateau, I turned to Alan, patted him on the back and said, 'Well, this is it, mate. Let's hope we can raise lots of money for Macmillan Nurses.'

'What about me?' Nick called out.

'Are you riding for charity as well?' I asked.

'Yes, I'm riding for the Arthritis Society, and the way my back is playing up this week, I might be needing their services by the time we finish the ride.'

Alan found a trail that led part way down the cliffs and called out, 'Why don't we collect a rock each, then throw them into the North Sea at John O'Groats?'

'What do you want to do that for?' asked Nick.

'I don't know really. Just for fun. As a gesture to link two remote enclaves together?'

'I worry about you sometimes. You've been hanging around with Ali too long.'

Nick scurried up the path while Alan and I chose two granite rocks and ascended towards the summit. As we approached Nick's bike, Alan opened one of the panniers, took out a bundle of clothes, located an unused compartment, and placed his small rock inside. I followed suit, as he quickly explained with a wink, 'He rarely cleans out his luggage. Let's see how far he carries them for us.'

Nick returned from a public toilet and asked, 'Are you done admiring my panniers and taking photos of the view? It's getting late, and in case you'd forgotten, we have a bike ride ahead of us, followed by a night of luxury at the hostel.'

My heart missed a beat as I remembered about the YHA. In the manic lead up to the ride, I had forgotten to book us in. As Nick bent down to inspect his sprockets, I excused myself for the toilet and sprinted towards the post office in search of Ron the postmaster. Without delay, he lent me his Yellow Pages, and while a new group of riders signed the official end-to-end logbook, I searched frantically for the number for the Youth Hostel Association. From a public phone booth, described on a plaque as the most westerly in England, I called the hotline and was put through to an operator.

'Hello, I hope you can help me. I'm after a family room for the YHA in Exeter for tomorrow night.'

'One moment, sir, please hold.'

As the phone fell silent, I looked through the window and could see them searching for me near the toilets.

'Hello, sir, I'm very sorry, but we only have dormitories available. Can I book this for you?'

I kicked the door and whispered an obscenity, then asked, 'How much would it cost to book the whole dormitory?'

'How many of you are there?'

'Three.'

'I'm afraid that's impossible. Besides the high cost, the room is filling up. We already have a group of four from London, plus an Italian. Tomorrow evening, we gain an Australian, so it looks like we will have a vibrant mix of international visitors. How marvellous!'

'What about breakfast? What do you have on the menu?'

'We offer healthy options these days, including organic muesli, fresh yoghurt and…'

Bang!

The window adjacent to my ear quivered, and I peered out to see them both staring at me from a few yards away. Nick opened the door and said sternly, 'Come on, we need to go.'

I nodded meekly, returned to the phone, and without further questions booked us in for the following night. As I replaced the receiver, I stared through the windows a final time. Nick was already on his bike, waiting by a faded white line that was painted in a straight line across the road. One side of the line said *Start*, the other said *Finish*.

A few tourists posed for photos, their legs straddling either side of the line, but as I trotted towards them, they stepped away and a young lad called out, 'Are you three about to cycle to John O'Groats?'

Nick pointed at me and replied sharply, 'We're trying to, mate, but this bloke keeps collecting rocks and phoning old girlfriends.'

And with that, he took the initiative, pushed down on his pedals, and started riding to Scotland. Alan followed suit. I waved goodbye to the tourists, then attempted to catch them up. An hour earlier we had been driven along this very road. But now it looked very different. For one thing, we were heading in the opposite direction. For another, we were finally pedalling.

The sedate hill that Matthew had coasted down in the car on the way to Land's End was no longer serene. I had teething problems within the first mile and could feel the panniers slipping on my right side because the material had been stretched during one of Nick's earlier exploits. As we passed through the first village, I dashed into a high street garage and purchased a set of bungee ropes from a chirpy receptionist. While handing over cash, the garage owner appeared, wearing his ginger sideburns with pride, and asked if I wanted any local cider to take away. I declined the offer and set off in search of my compatriots. With the panniers pinned into position, I eventually found my rhythm and tried to keep up as they zipped through village after village and forgot about waving to passersby.

The roads were hillier than I had envisaged, and as the afternoon wore on, I cursed myself for the lack of training I'd completed. The sedate lanes surrounding Land's End soon became a distant memory. We were now on the A30, a major roadway through Cornwall, swelled by holiday traffic, and as the angle of ascent increased, so too did the gap between us.

On each hill, Alan and Nick disappeared from sight, only to appear at the top, waiting patiently as I fought to find my rhythm and breath. Panting hard, I sucked on the warm air and tried to look relaxed, but my flushed cheeks and sweaty brow revealed all. I had no idea if they were secretly cursing my lack of fitness, but if they were, I wouldn't have blamed them. They slowed a little and I attempted to slipstream for the first time in my life. A few times it worked and I managed to stay focused, my eyes glued to Alan's rear wheels, and hour-by-hour we edged closer to Newquay.

At a roadside café, Nick studied the map and found an alternative route to the A30. The final miles were completed in relative peace, free from freight traffic and caravans. Inquisitive cows lifted their heads and chewed, watching as we dashed past. Each bend in the road revealed new surprises. On the left, a tractor towing a rickety trailer was stacked dangerously high with freshly cut hay. A little further on and we encountered a small dog, barking ferociously from the safe side of the fence as it ran parallel with us. For a few seconds, it cantered along a muddy trail towards the corner of the property. As the fence line approached, it ceased snarling and quietly returned to the gate, its tail held high in a show of domination.

Once or twice we met cyclists approaching at speed from the opposite direction, acknowledging our presence with a show of their palms. Then came a house, followed by another, and suddenly we were in a village, seemingly uninhabited except for rows of parked cars on the high street. We sped through in seconds and once more found ourselves surrounded by watchful cows.

Another curve, this time to the left, and suddenly we were descending. The land fell away, revealing a panoramic snapshot of the Atlantic, shimmering in the distance. Alan and Nick sensed adventure and blitzed ahead, lured by the call of the ocean. I laughed out loud, then tucked my head towards the handlebars and followed in their wake. The Donegal Flyer zipped along the road as I fought the urge to slam on the brakes before each bend. Hedgerows blurred past, wind buffeted my smiling face, and cows listened to my whoops of laughter. I had made it to the end of day one.

Newquay is the surfing capital of England and a mecca for those seeking a vibrant summer holiday. The focal point is the wide, pristine sands of Fistral Beach, pounded at its edge by the Atlantic.

As we cycled nearer, it was refreshing to see that not everyone under thirty years old escaped to the Mediterranean for their annual holiday. The main car park, that day, was filled with second-hand VW camper vans and throngs of teenagers, dressed in bathers and wetsuits after a day by the ocean. Families strolled past, weighed down by wet towels, beach balls, buckets and spades, in search of warm showers followed by fish and chips.

Out at sea, the last surfers of the day braved feisty waves, their bodies silhouetted by the setting sun. I wondered how many of these surfers would stick around for autumn, when low-pressure systems build up in the Atlantic Ocean, creating monster waves close to Fistral Beach. They are known as Cribbar and are dangerous, unpredictable and very powerful. To surf at Newquay is one thing. To surf the Cribbar earns your status in the surfing affinity.

If the Atlantic had been closer, I would have run barefoot into the foamy shoreline, but the wide expanse of sand was a barrier too far after such a long day. I observed the water's edge with weary eyes and turned towards the beachfront in search of Matthew, who had arranged to meet us. We located him by an ice cream van, chatting with a group of backpackers, and as we cycled nearer, he greeted us with good news.

He had booked us into a bed and breakfast and located our friend, Steve.

After a long, slow, burning hot shower, I emerged into our bedroom and sorted through my panniers to find something for the evening. Newquay was crammed with holidaymakers, and although I had trouble walking, I was still capable of talking and wanted to enjoy the night. The bungee ropes had squashed most of my clothes, and ironing seemed too much effort, so a creased shirt and shorts had to suffice.

Nick emerged from the shower room, wearing a crinkle-proof Hawaiian shirt, sailing shorts, and canvas sandals; I didn't look out of place alongside him. Alan appeared a few minutes later, whistling as he sprayed himself with deodorant and busied himself by the window. Then magically, he pulled from his panniers a navy shirt, free from a single crease, and perfectly folded jeans.

I stared at his outfit and asked, 'How did you do that?'

He stopped whistling for a second, added a dab of aftershave and said, 'You gotta be prepared for a night on the town. You should know that by now.'

8

Day 2: Road to Hell

"Because I want to; because I must; because now and forever more, this is where I belong to be."
    —Daphne du Maurier, Jamaica Inn

Newquay to Exeter (89 miles)

Our friend Steve was a changed man, both physically and mentally, since his move to Newquay. The outdoor life suited him. Although nearer to thirty than twenty, he was blessed with a shock of blonde, wavy hair, now bleached by the sun. His slim frame was solid, and he wore a permanent smile while nodding to bar owners and café workers as we sauntered along the cobbled back streets.

'So this is Newquay,' he announced with an air of authority and took us on a pub tour of the town. By midnight, I began to feel old. The pubs had shut and we were in a nightclub, shouting over pulsating music in an attempt to be heard. The clientele were in their late teens or early twenties, gyrating under flashing lights, and cavorting in the shadows. Steve and Matthew were deep in conversation with a local surf champion, Nick was contemplating another round of drinks, Alan had disappeared, and I was in need of a bed.

We staggered into bed in the early hours and lay like dead men. Matthew was the only one to rise with the sun, as he had to drive home, and shook us one by one until he heard grunts of disapproval. Breakfast was a quiet affair, broken by requests for water, juice, and more tea. Our cooked breakfast was served by a teenage waitress, who didn't hover at the table too long, except to collect orders for additional toast.

While we consumed our breakfast, I gazed through the window into the nearby street where smiling children ran past, dressed in bathers and floppy hats. Parents followed closely — carrying bags, deck chairs, buckets and spades — as they made their way to the beach.

We emerged from the bed and breakfast into clear skies, the warm sun shining brightly on our bikes. With reluctance, I strapped the panniers onto the Donegal Flyer and settled myself onto the saddle. Matthew came over and wished us good luck. He had just heard on the radio that it was going to be one of the hottest days of summer, and drove away with a knowing grin and a toot of the horn.

As he left the car park, Alan asked quietly, 'Well, Nick, which way?'

And so we set off to Exeter, 82 miles away, for a night in a dormitory. Within the first hour, I regretted the Tequila Slammers and the raucous group of women that appeared magically at our side when Steve ordered another tray of drinks to toast our health. I was also now lamenting the ensuing dancing session, with an unexpected 80s flurry, that sent us into a tailspin as we took over the dance floor until midnight.

The after-effects were brutal, and during the road trip from Cornwall to Devon, the A30 became the road to hell. All roads out of Newquay point skywards, and it was with determined ignorance that I cycled each and every hill and refused to walk during the eight-hour ride. I had no idea how Alan and Nick were feeling. I was too involved in my own pain to ask, but within a few hours, we settled into a steady pace along the A30.

We had stocked up on water but consumed it rapidly as rising temperatures sapped our strength. It wasn't just the heat that wore us down. The main problem was the close proximity of the cars, caravans, and lorries as they hurtled past, sucking us into their slipstream as we fought for control of the bikes. After too many close encounters, I dealt with this problem by steering towards the verge as they approached, but this was also fraught with difficulties.

From a car window you would never know that the breakdown strip is a minefield of discarded car parts, squashed animals, broken glass, and shredded tyres. In one stretch, which shall forever be known to me as *Suicide Alley*, a cumbersome caravan created a backlog of frustrated drivers, forcing me into the danger zone. During this two-mile section, the bitumen was littered with stones, rusted exhaust pipes, cats' eyes (man-made), a TV screen, numerous dead rabbits, and hundreds of red plastic intrusions drilled into the surface. These, I presume, were designed to alert tired drivers that they were about to drive onto Bodmin Moor.

From time to time, I would glance up in an attempt to take in the serene beauty of the wild moors, but like an exhausted child at Disney, I was incapable of appreciating the view. Our unexpected saviour for the day was a building dating back to 1750. For hundreds of years, the Jamaica Inn has welcomed weary travellers, and its location, on the edge of the moorland, was a beguiling sight.

In 1930, a writer called Daphne du Maurier stayed at the inn, and during her first morning, went horse riding on the moors with a friend, becoming hopelessly lost in a blanket of mist. Thankfully, they recovered from the ordeal and decided to stay at the inn for a few more days. During this period, the fireside tales of ghosts, rum smugglers, and local skullduggery inspired her to write a fictional story about the illegal activities of Cornish pirates and rogues. She named her book *Jamaica Inn*. Nine years later, it was turned into a film and directed by Alfred Hitchcock.

Like many historical buildings, the Jamaica Inn has earned a reputation over the centuries for being haunted. Maybe the bumps in the night, heard by overnight guests, are the imagination of weary travellers, or just the creaking of ancient timbers as they settle.

At the rear of the inn, we discovered a large, cobblestone beer garden and searched for an empty table among patrons enjoying the summer sun. Most people looked very relaxed as they clinked glasses, shared stories, and studied the all-day menu.

We found a vacant table near the rear of the garden, and as soon as the bikes were propped against the wall, Nick dropped to his knees on the ground and then silently rolled onto his back.

'What are you doing?' I asked.

'It's his dodgy back. You'll get used to it,' explained Alan between gulps of water. Apart from a trickle of sweat on his brow, he looked unscathed by the A30 and was keen to order food and refreshments. We left Nick on the floor and headed towards the door of the back bar, known as the Smugglers Inn. I knew that my face was flushed from exertion and each step was mechanical, as though my legs had forgotten the art of walking in a straight line. Maybe that's why we earned a few chuckles as we stiffly walked past those that had arrived at the inn without breaking into a sweat.

The interior was cool, dark, and welcoming. Exposed beams on the low ceiling added an air of authenticity to the décor, and the walls were decorated with memorabilia about the inn's historic past. For a fleeting moment, I considered booking a haunted room for the night and snuggling onto a cushioned seat by the inglenook with a good book, maybe a ploughman's lunch, and a pot of ale.

While Alan studied the real ale section, the barman came over and greeted us. He was about thirty years of age, with a mop of curly hair and a dashing smile. I was hoping for a surly barman with weather-beaten features and bushy eyebrows, who would lean across the bar and whisper, 'Don't travel across the moors. Not tonight! Strange things have been happening around these parts. It isn't safe, I tell you.'

Instead, the barman smiled cheerfully, and in an Australian twang, asked, 'G'day, lads. What can I getcha?'

While beers were being poured, we ordered three portions of lamb stew and admired the décor. The owners of the inn were obviously proud of its heritage, with plaques and pictures of yesteryear lining the plastered walls.

During the 17th and 18th century, coaching inns played a vital role for travellers and were located on major roads across Europe. Many have now been demolished or have fallen into disrepair. Some were saved and converted into theme pubs or restaurants.

The Jamaica Inn still offers overnight rooms, and its remote setting on the edge of Bodmin Moor adds a touch of mystery that you will not find in a Travelodge!

If time travel were ever invented and you only had one chance to try it out, I would choose to go back in time to the 1600s. Imagine the stories, once told in establishments like the Jamaica Inn, from those that had travelled across the moors by horse and carriage. The talk would be about highwaymen, how many shillings for a bed, how far to Exeter, the state of the road, and local gossip.

Nowadays, the first words that I often hear from patrons when they visit a roadside eatery is, 'Do you have free Wi-Fi?'

I opted out of a haunted room for the night and carried a pint of beer to Nick, who was now fiddling with the front wheel of the Donegal Flyer.

'I wondered why you were struggling so much. You've pinged two spokes,' he declared as I came closer.

I remembered that the wheel had felt wonky, but had put it down to delirium. Broken spokes were something I had never encountered. Nick busied himself with tools, pulled two spare spokes from his panniers, and within minutes, my wheels were spinning perfectly.

'Cheers, mate,' I said and raised my glass.

'Anytime, but please don't break anymore until we get to Exeter. They were the only spares I had.'

When lunch was finished, we pushed our bikes towards the road in order to reconvene. Nick stopped abruptly, looked down at his wheels, and swore softly to himself.

'What is it?' I asked.

'I've got two broken spokes.'

The remaining hours were completed in relative silence. Nick's bike limped along, Alan took the lead, and I remained at the rear. As the sun beat down from a cloudless sky, I no longer swerved towards the verge upon hearing the sound of approaching lorries. It was too arduous.

Instead, I thought about mum and what she would have said about my adventure. She had always enjoyed a good yarn, and I hoped she would have been proud. I found myself daydreaming, thinking back to the time when she was alive — the kitchen at dinnertime, filled with five hungry teenagers, searching for doorstop wedges of freshly cut bread, strategically placed on the table to keep us at bay while she slaved over the cooker. Sitting on the front porch, enjoying cups of tea with neighbours, and her shrill laugh as she learned the antics of eccentric locals.

A car horn snapped me back to reality when I swerved towards the edge, and I concentrated once more on pedalling in a straight line. I counted out a hundred revolutions and then tried counting to a thousand. But there was always a distraction and I rarely finished. Maybe it was a discarded wheel, a mangled rabbit, or a quick glance to see how far Nick and Alan were ahead. I started counting to another thousand, gave up halfway through and looked up.

They had pulled over to stop, and as I approached, I could now see why. They were standing underneath the *Welcome to Exeter* signpost with their arms held wide.

We followed signs for the town and searched for bike shops, but the few that we found were now closed. As Nick scouted the area, I called the YHA to confirm our booking and to find the exact location.

Their phone answered on the first ring, 'Oh yes, we know you're coming. But we're not actually in town. It's not far by car though.'

'We're not in cars,' I explained irritably. 'We're on bikes and have just ridden over 82 miles from Newquay.'

'Oh, how splendid. You must be so fit.'

'Not really, I'm just knackered, actually,' I heard myself say.

She ignored my remark and advised, 'Well, if you're in town, all you have to do now is ride down the Topsham Road. It's a lovely main road, and it's downhill from where you are. We're near the river mouth.'

I felt such a fool. Not only was it not in town, but also further south, which meant that we would have to backtrack up the Topsham Road in the morning.

I cycled over to where Nick and Alan sat on a park bench, waiting impatiently for their long hot showers.

'Well there is good news and bad news,' I explained.

'The good news is that the YHA has an amazing setting, adjacent to a country park with river frontage. The bad news, is that you have to follow me without hurling any abuse, because it's just a touch out of town.'

And with that, I set off at pace down the Topsham Road, hoping that the Australian backpacker wasn't going to snore all night. The receptionist was a sprightly young girl, with short, dark hair and a friendly smile. She wasn't wearing a Ban the Bomb T-shirt, and she dressed very plainly, for which I was eternally grateful. Nick was unusually quiet and mooched in the doorway, stretching his back into many angles, as though he were trying to escape from an invisible web.

'Now, sir, are you all members?' she asked. 'If not, you can get a 20% discount off your bill if you join tonight.'

The temptation was there, but I could sense that a lynching was on the cards if my fellow travellers didn't find their room soon.

'Maybe in the morning,' I said.

'OK, sir, your room is just down on the left. It's dormitory number three. You can't miss it. Take your pick of any of the spare beds.'

Alan's eyes widened, then he nodded slowly and made a soft chuckling sound. Nick had not heard a thing and picked up his panniers as we made our way along the corridor. I entered first, hoping to find a small dormitory, filled with empty beds.

It held eight bunks, which meant sixteen beds. At least half were already taken. Clothes, bags and boots were scattered around the base of some beds, and the unmade white sheets glared under the fluorescents lights.

I noticed a large Italian football shirt draped over the side of a bottom bunk. The owner would be a stout man, and I decided to steer clear of the vacant top bed, in case he wriggled and fidgeted in the night.

I stepped over a discarded water bottle, caught Nick scowling at me, and announced, 'Well, this is cosy'.

He removed his glasses, surveyed the room and through gritted teeth, said; 'I see you failed to book a family room then.'

I attempted a smile and replied, 'I haven't slept in a top bunk since I was a kid.'

Nick grimaced and in a low voice, mumbled, 'I swear…'

'Bagsy this one,' Alan called out and placed his panniers on an unclaimed bottom bunk.

'I bagsy bailing out and finding a bed and breakfast!' Nick proclaimed, 'but I'm too tired to move.' And with that, he sat on the nearest available bed, while I clambered onto the top bunk opposite.

For a few minutes there was silence, then the creak of a bedspring, followed by the sound of whistling as Alan headed to the communal shower and called, 'Cheer up, lads, I think we've earned ourselves a beer.'

By the second drink, Nick had calmed. After dinner, Alan convinced us to try the local cider, but as the evening wore on, stifled yawns and weary legs forced an end to the night. It was close to midnight when we rang the buzzer to the YHA. A night warden appeared at the door and whispered, 'No noise now. It's way too late. You lads are in the dorm, right?'

'Yes, mate, for one night only,' Nick replied as we made our way down the corridor. I pushed open the doorway, expecting to see the room exactly as we had left it hours before. But it was plunged into darkness, and from the snorts and grumbles permeating from the room, now filled with people. Where had they all been earlier? I had no idea, but as we stood by the doorway trying to remember the location of our beds, Nick whispered something about nocturnal bird watchers.

Then I heard a noise that struck me with dread, and I knew at that very moment that it was going to be a long night unless I could locate my earplugs. But even with pieces of foam inserted into my ear canals, I was guessing that the awful sound emitting from the mystery snorer would penetrate my defences.

Sharing a room with a human foghorn was not something I had envisaged when we set off from Newquay fourteen hours earlier, but as we stood by the doorway, hoarse gasps resonated around us, as our offending room mate sucked in large quantities of the stale air. I was guessing he was a big man; he was certainly dependable. I calculated that he snored three times a minute.

For a few moments, we fumbled in the shadows, keeping the dormitory door partially open to allow a shard of light from the passageway into the room. I tiptoed past a series of sleepers and while locating my bed, heard the scrape of a plastic bag, followed by a sound that sounded like someone tripping. Somewhere in the darkness, there was a suppressed chuckle that could only be Alan's.

Nick's voice cut through the darkness as he whispered, 'It's no good. I'm turning the light on.'

From another direction, someone called out, 'Shush!'

From afar, I heard more giggles from Alan.

Then another voice, this one sterner than the first, 'Pipe down, it's the middle of the night.'

Click. The room was flooded with light. The mystery snorer let out a loud splutter, his Italian shirt now on the floor, and his bronze face partially hidden by a thin sheet.

I moved to my bunk and scrambled up the steps, all thoughts of dental hygiene forgotten as I dived onto the top bed.

'Turn that bloody light out,' a grizzled voice called.

From an unknown source, came a high pitched reply, 'There's a war on you know.'

From my vantage point, I watched Nick as he discarded his clothes, pulled back the sheets, lay down, and mummified himself in the blanket. Further away, Alan was having problems, and I sat up to investigate. His voice was raised and I could hear the conversation clearly.

'Excuse mate, but that's my bed.'

'Bugger off, it's mine.'

'But I was here a few hours ago and left my...'

'Strewf, mate. Just clear off and find your own bloody bed.'

'I'll tell you what', Alan said, 'I'll leave you in peace in your special bed. But just to let you know, I left my underpants and T-shirt under my, sorry, your pillow. Plus, my panniers are stuffed in the gap underneath, so I'm going to rummage around for a bit.'

'Lights off, please!' a strained voice called.

'Never again,' Nick announced and rolled over.

'Thanks, mate,' Alan said and reached under the man's head, retrieved his underpants, and went in search of a new bed.

'Lights!' said another roommate.

'Camera, action,' replied the high-pitched joker once more.

I suppressed a giggle and lay flat, my head spinning with fatigue and the after-effects of too much cider. I pulled the covers over my head in an attempt to mask the glare and waited for the light to get switched off. For a few moments there was silence, apart from the thunderous eruptions from the Italian foghorn. Nothing, I decided, would wake him. Then unexpectedly I heard the stomp of feet towards the light switch, and with an accompanying 'Bloody cyclists!' the room was plunged into darkness.

As the mystery light switcher returned to his bed, I heard a clip as he tripped over Nick's discarded panniers, wailed in pain for a brief moment, and then found his bed. I stuck my head out of the sheets and listened once more. Just as calm prevailed, Alan softly called out, 'Night lads.'

Somewhere in the darkness, came a high-pitched reply, 'Night night, John Boy!'

In between the Italian's rhythmic snores, I could just make out a faint chuckle as I drifted off to sleep.

Nick's bed.

9

Day 3: I Don't Like Mondays

"It does not matter how slowly you go, as long as you do not stop."
— **Confucius**

Exeter to Cheddar (59 miles)

By morning they were all gone — the comedian, the Australian, the Italian, and the mystery light switcher. I secretly prayed that breakfast would be a sumptuous affair, but alas, it was all that Nick expected. By the time we made our way to the dining hall, the remainder of the cooked buffet was tepid or charred, and the thought of organic muesli didn't sit well for any of us.

I couldn't help feeling that if I had booked a family room, the outcome would have been very different. Hostels are amazing places, filled with travellers from across the world. Get it right and you can stay in castles, stately homes, and funky cottages by the beach. But we were grouchy and less appreciative than normal after the long ride from Newquay, and the unsettled night had left us edgy.

We thanked the receptionist, and ventured outside. Dappled clouds and a bracing wind had replaced the blue skies, and we silently departed in search of a café and spare spokes. Nick found a bike shop, stocked up on supplies, and repaired his wheel using a public bench in the pedestrianised zone. I supplied egg and bacon rolls, washed down with freshly ground coffee, while Alan studied the map.

It was a Monday morning and the streets were already filled with shoppers, carrying throwaway plastic bags filled with food or clothes. Many pedestrians were dressed for rain and traipsed the streets, snuggled up in jackets, jeans and trainers. A funky coffee shop, decorated with travel posters of faraway places, enjoyed brisk trade as groups of mums eagerly exchanged stories between sips of cappuccino and persistent checks on babies sleeping in nearby pushers. Two stools by the window were claimed by an elderly couple, quietly nursing their warm drinks and seemingly oblivious to the ceaseless gibber of the mums on the adjacent table.

It struck me that we were watching a snippet of what happened on a typical Monday in Exeter High Street. It wasn't extraordinary, but it was real. Friends meeting to share stories, make plans, enjoy lunch, shop, or pass the time of day. Our world, for a short time, offered no such regular conformity, and a week from now, when the mums and toddlers group met once more, we would be somewhere in Scotland. With this thought bouncing around in my head, I waved to the elderly couple and went in search of Alan.

'I have a plan', he announced. 'The village of Cheddar is about seventy miles away, and there's a town called Bridgewater halfway, where we can grab a few beers and lunch. If we leave soon, we should be in Cheddar for teatime.' He then swallowed two painkillers, washed down with water. I'd noticed that he was taking them each morning since leaving Torquay and decided to ask why.

His answer was simplistic. 'You know how it is. Too many football injuries, completing the London Marathon with very little training and a stubbornness to get medical attention. So for now, it's a case of smiling, taking the pills twice a day, and riding to the next town.' His dodgy knee was never mentioned again.

Nick had repaired his bike and called out, 'All good to go! Alan, lead the way, mate.'

We set off at pace and headed onto the ring road, leaving the clouds behind as we rode inland towards blue skies and the town of Cheddar. Our pace all morning was relentless. It was as though my compatriots were keen to put Exeter out of their mind. After a brief stop for pies and roadside tea, the pace eased a little, and as we set off once again, Nick reached into his front bag, pulled out a small piece of card, and declared, 'OK, lads, it's time to play Trivial Pursuit.'

The roads were busy with the usual mix of caravans, lorries and commuters, and we had cycled in single file since leaving Exeter, but a quick look behind revealed a gap with no traffic. For a few seconds, we rode three abreast, while Nick asked the first question, 'Where would you find the Sea of Tranquility?'

The sound of approaching traffic triggered a brisk return to single file, where we deliberated the answer. Surprisingly, the game worked well, and by the time we reached Bridgewater, we had managed to use up three cards!

During our pub lunch, I discussed an idea for an additional game that we could use when the moment arose, to supplement the Trivial

Pursuit idea. As the empty plates were stacked onto the end of the table, I asked, 'How many countries will we cycle through on our trip?'

'Three, of course,' Nick replied.

'What about counties?' I then asked.

'Haven't got a clue?' Alan said.

'What about towns, villages and cities?'

'What are you thinking?' Nick asked.

'When I was a kid, we used to play a game where the first person to reach a new place earned a point. Maybe we can invent a similar game for this trip.'

They stared at me, grinning lightly, as I attempted to explain the rules.

'What if we earn one point for the first person to reach a village, five points for a town, ten for a county border, ten also for the evenings destination, and twenty for a new country?'

'What does the winner get?' asked Nick.

'I don't know. Maybe the winner each day gets the first choice of bed for that evening.'

Alan's eyes were wide as he said, 'But your bike isn't as fast, and without sounding funny, you're not fit enough to race us yet.'

'That's OK. I'll take my chances and may even get a win from time to time. Remember the tortoise and the hare!'

To be truthful, I was just glad that they agreed to give it a go. There were no real rules as such, but it was just another diversion that would help us when the times got tough, and a few hours later, I was glad for the challenge.

Nick handpicked a quiet road to Cheddar, and we found ourselves on a glorious stretch of countryside where the road dipped and curved for mile after mile. When a village appeared in the distance, Alan or Nick raced each other to the finishing line at the signpost. I followed in their wake, found out the winner, and made a mental note of the leader's board.

Between bouts of Trivial Pursuit, racing to villages, and snippets of chitchat, the afternoon passed quickly. It was late afternoon when a blackboard menu, displaying homemade cream teas at a thatched café, tempted us to stop and eat. While my friends deliberated over the menu, I sneaked a peek at Nick's map. If my calculation was correct, we were not far from the Somerset border, and they seemed oblivious to this fact.

When it was time for our departure, they headed towards the counter to pay, and I ran towards the Donegal Flyer, climbed onboard and started riding. After a few minutes, the temptation to look behind became too hard to ignore, and as I turned my head, I could distinctly see them far behind. I concentrated hard, pushing my legs as fast as they could go, and searched up ahead for the county sign. The angle of the road changed once more, and I felt the first pang of defeat as the uphill incline reduced my speed.

I chanced another glimpse behind, and my heart sunk. Alan was approaching fast. I arrived at the top of the slope and was sure that up ahead there was a road sign. With no idea what it said, I gave a final push and rode hard, not daring to look behind.

It was a large, black and white sign, positioned by two poles sunk deep into the earth. Emblazoned in the middle were the words, *Welcome to Somerset,* and I swept past with my arms wide in salute. Alan passed me within seconds, revealing a wide grin and shouting, 'Double bed for you tonight!'

The parish of Cheddar turned out to be an endearing location. Nestled on the edge of the Mendip Hills, the village manages to maintain its character, despite the fact that the nearby gorge attracts 500,000 visitors every year. Cheddar Gorge was formed over a million years ago, as melt-water from the ice-age eroded the limestone, and today it is described as one of Britain's natural wonders. As we cycled towards the village, we discussed the idea of booking into a bed and breakfast and then cycling through the gorge, which in places is 449 feet deep.

But the moment we found a bed and breakfast and set our panniers down on the bedroom carpet, a wave of exhaustion fell upon us. We were invited for tea by the owner and sat quietly on a leather couch as she poured drinks and gave an impromptu lecture on the wealth of attractions in the area. We nodded appreciatively, but all I could think about was a warm shower to ease the severe ache in my buttocks, and although the Cheddar cheese factory sounded appealing, I was glad it was now shut for the day.

Without asking, she topped up our cups and next informed us about the nearby gorge, where they had discovered a human male skeleton dating back to 7150BC.

'They named him Cheddar Man,' she declared proudly. 'You should go and take a look at where he was found.' But exhaustion had sapped our curiosity, and the only place we wanted to find was one that offered hot food and refreshments.

A walk through the village revealed numerous clues that tourists flocked to the area. Café windows were decorated with flyers of caving excursions, cottages offered cream teas, and a poster in the window of the closed post office declared, *Mystery Tour on Monday. Limited seats. Book Here!*

Despite the fact that so many people visit here each year, we struggled to find many of them. There were certainly no obvious international visitors with expensive cameras, guidebooks and maps. Maybe no one went out after 8.30pm on Mondays, or they were still on the mystery tour.

When we entered the first pub, we were informed that due to the late hour (it was 8.37pm on the clock by the counter) that food was no longer being served. The Indian restaurant, however, was open until midnight. So with this in mind, we sampled a few local ciders then went in search of a curry. During the meal, the subject of spare clothes was mentioned, which led to a conversation about Nick's wife's trip to Scotland and I asked, 'So tell us more about her friend, Sam?'

Nick put down his fork and said, 'Well, as you know, I introduced her to my mate, and soon after, they were married. That was years ago. Now she's single and has been for some time. She's quite a catch, Karen reckons. But it will take a certain type of man to tame her.'

'What do you mean?' I asked.

Nick thought about this for a moment and said carefully, 'She is spirited, Ali.'

Then he added, 'You'll both like her and she loves spicy food.'

He then ordered three more pints of Kingfisher and another basket of poppadoms.

10

Day 4: Breathe

"It makes no difference if I burn my bridges behind me. I never retreat."
— **Fiorello LaGuardia**

Cheddar to Hereford (82 miles)

'Delicious,' Nick exclaimed as the landlady offered more bacon and topped up his teacup.

'Try the marmalade, dear. I make my own you know. If you don't mind me asking, where exactly are you cycling to?'

'John O'Groats,' he replied proudly

'That's a long way for one day!' she exclaimed.

'Oh, no, that's our final destination,' he explained. 'Today we're heading to Wales via the Severn Bridge, then onto Hereford.'

She looked over at her husband, who was busy with the crosswords, and said, 'We know a shortcut to the bridge, don't we, Ernie?'

He looked up and asked, 'What's that, my dear?'

'A shortcut to the bridge. We know one, don't we?'

Nick was all ears and scurried off in search of his map.

'You won't be needing that!' she declared as he walked back into the dining room.

'This is a local road. You won't find it in one of those things.'

How a sealed road would fail to make it on an AA map intrigued me, unless of course it was constructed after 1975, and I was beginning to have reservations on the credibility of her claim. But while she brewed more tea and offered fresh pancakes, there was no disputing that she was a relaxing alternative to our YHA experience.

'It's easy,' she declared.

'Drive out of the gate and keep left past the farm. But you don't want to take the road with the signpost. That's what the tourists use.

Keep going a bit further, past Albert's piggery, and then turn left at the phone box. The lane is a bit steep, but we drive it most weeks, don't we, Ernie?'

I felt myself stammering as I quickly asked, 'Excuse me, you're talking about driving up the hill in your car, but... but we're on bikes.'

'It's all the same by me.' she muttered. 'Bikes are allowed as well. We all pay our taxes.'

'No, I meant that cars have engines, but bikes just have chains and pedals.'

She looked at me quizzically and said, 'I won't tell a soul that you used the road. It's our secret.'

Ernie excused himself to dig up potatoes, and while she cleared the plates, Nick hurried off to pack. As we waved goodbye, he announced, 'What a find. This will easily shave an hour off the ride.' I hoped he was right.

We never found Albert's piggery, but did locate a phone box and turned into the lane. Within a few seconds, the angle rose steeply and we soon entered a shadowy world, as trees from each side of the road spread their canopy overhead. The sharp angle forced us into single file, just as Alan called out from the front, 'Don't forget, walking isn't allowed.'

And so it began. The shortest, hardest ride of my life took twenty minutes, and with each revolution of the pedals, the temptation to walk grew stronger. There were no cars, just us, on a winding road through a pocket of woodland. Each bend bought hope, but around each corner, another twisted incline would appear. Alan had vanished, Nick was at the edge of my vision, and I remained at the back, concentrating solely on my pedals.

Sweat continually trickled into my eyes and hindered my vision. I wiped them with the back of my hand, gained a moment of respite, and had a sudden flashback to *Rocky III*, where he is getting beaten to a pulp, but refuses to drop and shouts to Clubber Lang, 'Ain't so bad, ain't so bad.'

Now I was muttering those same words, over and over again — head down, bum up — as I cranked the pedals and refused to walk. I looked up from the road and found myself adjacent with the right hand verge, subconsciously taking the quickest way around the bend with little thought for oncoming traffic. I snapped back to reality, wiped my eyes once more, and swerved back into the left lane.

The trees diminished, replaced by blackberry bushes and coarse scrubland clinging to a grassy knoll, but the acute angle of ascent rarely altered. I was in the lowest gear possible, but the tension on the chain was unbearable as my leg muscles screamed for respite.

I no longer thought of Rocky. I was unable to think of anything except walking or, better still, lying down on the road. Up ahead I could see another bend in the road, and the concept of dismounting crowded my thoughts. What would it matter? Alan and Nick would never know, and I could probably run alongside my bike quicker than I could cycle. I decided right there and then to dismount.

The pain was too intense and who would care? But I was halfway around the corner and couldn't find the will to lift my leg over the saddle. I made the turn and something weird happened: the tension on the pedals eased slightly. I looked up then, and yards away were Alan and Nick, lying spread-eagled on a patch of grass. We had reached the summit.

Alan's flushed face told me all that I needed to know about how he was feeling, and in between gulps of water, he spluttered something about unusual shortcuts. Nick was standing nearby, his shirt drenched in sweat as he studied the map. As I dismounted and rolled onto the grass, he announced cheerfully, 'Well, that was a good way to wake us up, and what a magnificent view.'

I lifted my head, glanced at the scenery, and grunted in agreement. Even from my acute angle, it was true, England looked glorious. The landscape rippled with villages, and small towns nestled in each contour. Rows of hedgerows segregated the patchwork of green fields, and in the distance, a solitary tractor chugged along a farmyard track. In the adjacent meadow, a handful of swifts hunted for insects, continually swooping and darting above the long grass in a final feeding frenzy before their long migration to Equatorial and Southern Africa.

Within a few weeks, they would be undertaking one of the longest migratory journeys in the world, flying 14,000 miles across oceans and deserts, to return to their feeding grounds. They didn't need maps to guide them. Their homing skills were far more precise, and with luck, they would return to the Mendip Hills the following year.

In comparison to their epic trip, all we had to do for the remainder of the day was cross the Severn Bridge, traverse the Wye Valley, and locate a bed and breakfast. With luck, our feeding ground would be a pub in Hereford, selling refreshing ales and West Country steaks.

The shortcut elated Nick, who was now convinced that the remainder of the day would be gloriously easy. I still wasn't exactly sure what the diversion had omitted from our original plan, but for the view alone, it had been worth it. I was tempted to take a look at the map to find our location, but I was still trying to catch my breath. It was to remain a secret, and after a few minutes' respite, Nick was impatient and began to ride in circles on the road, calling us up from the floor to commence once more.

With considerable ease, we traversed onto the A38, blitzed towards Bristol, took the bypass, and followed our noses towards the River Severn. The midday sky was dotted with altocumulus clouds, their grey-white features peppering the skyline. To our left, the wide, lazy waters of the River Severn split the land. Far on the other side, was the country of Wales, and linking the banks were two bridges. The oldest and northernmost bridge was part of the M48, and for many decades, was the main freight route between England and Wales. Thirty years later, due to increased traffic, a new bridge was opened a few miles downriver and is now the main link to Wales, as part of the M4 motorway system. The original bridge was constructed in 1966 to replace a car ferry operation that had been running for decades. I have no idea what happened to the boats, or those that relied on the trade for their livelihood, but the crumbling car ramp still remains.

I contemplated how it must have felt to be part of the riverside crossing when the bridge was being constructed — looking up from the water, knowing that your livelihood and a way of life was about to end once the ribbon was cut. Did the ferry remain open for a while, hoping that drivers would stay faithful?

My guess is that trade dropped sharply, as drivers chose the speediest option available. Is that what life is now? Hurtling from one place to another as fast as possible, in order to save time? But what do we do with this additional time? Do we use it to relax or to undertake something special with family? Or do we attempt to stuff even more into each day?

During the last few years, I had been guilty of cramming too much into my waking hours, and my wrinkled brow showed the signs. Since Mum had died, I had found relaxation difficult, but I sensed a change occurring.

The ride unearthed an additional treasure — and that was time to think. Yes, we had to keep to an approximate schedule, but as long as we cycled an average of 70 miles per day, we would reach our goal. Playing Trivial Pursuit, chatting alongside Alan and Nick, then racing to claim new towns was just a part of our day. The remaining time gave me the chance to reflect, and it became for me a form of meditation.

I thought back to my teenage years and felt a pang of guilt at the lost opportunities when I should have helped pull my weight. Mum was a single parent, raising five children between the ages of twelve and twenty. Our household was a lively residence and as *Madness* once sang, "there's always something happening, and it's usually quite loud."

On a typical Saturday evening, the stairs were constantly pounded in both directions as everyone prepared for their evening. Barney the dog may have escaped to terrorise unsuspecting passersby, Alice claimed the bathroom, while Matthew played vinyl records in his bedroom. Michael and Dave paraded around in their new shirts, friends would loiter in the hallway, and during all this, Mum prepared dinner after working all day, selling bread and scones.

By my mid-teens, I had become apt at hanging out the washing and often shared laughs with Mum over cups of tea, but that was about as far as my helpfulness stretched. Over the following years, my sister was married, Michael discovered the nightlife of Chelsea, Dave purchased a house, and Barney disappeared (I think he was euthanised for biting pedestrians, but Mum said he had been stolen by gypsies). By the time I was 24, I was planning to move out to live with my girlfriend. Matthew would be the last remaining sibling at home.

Unbeknown to the family, Mum had been hiding a secret. She was suffering bouts of acute pain, and during a holiday to Ireland, her condition suddenly deteriorated. When at last the doctors checked her condition, it was deemed too late. The diagnosis was clear. She had terminal cancer, and not once during the extensive treatment to prolong her life and ease her pain did she complain. Alice became our rock, Michael returned from London, Dave was forever dependable, and Matthew and I grew up.

In the final stages of cancer, Macmillan nurses entered our home, and with angelic grace, cared for her until the end.

Years later, the hours in the saddle were giving me the space to put these emotional events into perspective. It was finally time for me to look forward, not behind. I snapped out of my diversionary thoughts and looked up to scan the road ahead. Alan and Nick were close by and had stopped to take photos. We were near the river's edge, and the two large bridges were visible from our vantage point.

Nick's map indicated that, for cyclists, the original bridge was the way to proceed, and it was here that we found ourselves on a windswept Tuesday. A designated walkway and cycle way hugged the left hand side of this bridge, and after navigating a few turnstiles (to prevent cars), we earned an optimum view of the estuary.

In places, the River Severn is five miles wide and is Britain's longest river system, at 220 miles long. It also has an unusual ecosystem, leading to tidal surges when conditions arise. They occur across the world in a small number of locations and are known as river bores. These powerful waves head upstream, and as the river narrows, the size and power of the swell increases to resemble a miniature tsunami.

One man, a local surfer known as Steve King, once surfed over seven miles on the river bore, and with increasing knowledge of the factors that trigger this rare phenomenon, they can now be accurately predicted. Those that attempt a river bore only have one chance to surf the main break, as there are rarely any other sets of waves behind the first one.

From our vantage point, the river looked to be a slow moving body of grey water, with small islands of mud peering out above the shallows. There were no signs of surfers waiting for freak waves, just a single boat chugging against the flow. We rode past suspension cables, painted iron grey, and I thought back to something my Dad had always said. "If you want a job for life, go and paint the Severn Bridge. As soon as they've finished, they start all over again because it takes so many years."

There were no signs of commercial painters swinging from ropes between the steel columns, but there was a group of cyclists up ahead, taking a group photo with a self-timer. We pulled over to assist and soon got chatting.

They were a group of four. Two were women, in their late twenties, and two were men, in their late teens. The chattiest of the group was a woman with a wild frizz of ginger hair, which she constantly tried to control as it whipped in front of her face. As she passed her camera over, she said, 'Thanks for that. We're cycling to Hereford.'

I took a quick snap and replied, 'Well, guess what? So are we.'

'How come?' she asked.

'Oh, we're cycling to John O'Groats,' I stated proudly.

Her green eyes widened, then she looked across at her group and declared, 'Well, so are we!'

For a few minutes, we traded questions and answers; each group was eager to share their exploits and secret spots. The wind played havoc, snatching words and causing miscommunication, and I could see that her friends were eager to depart.

We agreed to meet again, this time in Hereford.

'Where will we see you?' she asked.

'How about a pub in the town?' Alan said and then added, 'To make it easy, we can meet in a pub that has an animal in its name.'

'What if there isn't one?' one of the lads asked.

'This is England. We love pubs with quirky names. If there's nothing with an animal in it, then look for one with an odd sounding name. We'll be there.'

The lad looked at him blankly, so Alan explained, 'You know, like the Frog and Rhubarb, or the Pickle and Cucumber.'

He opened his mouth to say something, but was tapped on the shoulder by the ginger girl. 'Yes, we get it. See you there!' she exclaimed.

And then they were gone. As they set off, Nick chortled and said, 'I reckon the lads think we're after their women.'

Maybe he was right. But Nick was happily married, and from what I knew of Alan, the women did not seem his type. And I was eager to meet up with them only to see how they were faring. Being the slowest of the three was playing on my mind, and I was keen to talk with their weakest rider to ask what coping strategies they used. Did they also re-enact Rocky movies to motivate them on steep sections, or play Trivial Pursuit on quiet roads? Did they daydream or count pedal revolutions in the same way that children count sheep? Did they tire of the weaving caravans whizzing dangerously close as they sped by? Or for them, was it all a breeze? Was I missing a magical ingredient?

We were now over the halfway point of the bridge, and the impromptu stop had encouraged Nick to rummage around for his camera. While he snapped images from the comfort of his bike seat, I leant over to scan the water below. Now that we had stopped, it was possible to appreciate the powerful surge as this mighty river flowed strongly towards the sea. From a car window, I had often thought of the River Severn as a placid stretch of wide water, but could now appreciate that it was a major waterway, displacing millions of gallons per day.

Alan and Nick chatted incessantly as we commenced and were in no mood to overtake me. Desperate to enjoy the view, I meandered slowly and they tucked in behind with Nick snapping photos of pylons, sea gulls, and the estuary. As the road began dipping towards land, I ventured forward, my eyes seeking out the fertile shore for signs of wildlife. As we edged closer to shore, I could see small birds skipping over the mudflats and heard the call of a kingfisher as it took flight.

I was suddenly alone, and without thought, had picked up speed as the end of the bridge approached. It was at this time that I remembered that the River Severn was a natural border between England and Wales, and it suddenly struck me that a new country was only yards away and we had all forgotten. A sneak peek behind revealed Alan and Nick were still relaxed, their heads moving from side to side as they admired the surroundings and made small talk.

I crouched low, stamped hard, and rode directly into the wind, the estuary to my left, cars and trucks up high to my right. Pylons flashed past as I streaked along the empty track. Up ahead, I could see a sign. Was it the border for Wales? My heart skipped in anticipation. Within seconds, I was able to read the words: *Beware! Barrier Ahead.*

I slowed, but the barricade was nearer than envisaged and I yanked hard on my brake. The back wheel locked and then skidded, but thankfully I slowed in time to traverse a contra-flow around strategically placed, concrete barricades.

Just ahead was another sign, but I rushed forward. This one cautioned, *Beware of Painters Overhead.* I had no time to search for these mythical workers, and a shout from behind spurred me on. They were chasing me. I raced on, leaving the final pylon behind me, and there in front of me, in all its glory, was a signpost, welcoming me to Wales. I stopped underneath it, just as Alan and Nick whizzed past, their faces smiling.

Southern Wales was flatter than I envisaged. The wild, untamed Brecon Beacons, where the SAS undertake survival training, were far to the north. This was a gentle landscape, decorated by natural woodland, working farms and quiet villages. The only clues that we were in Wales were the dual language signposts.

I have the utmost admiration for those that are bilingual, and the Welsh language has made resurgence in recent years with many local schools now including it in their curriculum. UNESCO has a multitude of information concerning the fate of the world's languages. According to their website, the Welsh language is deemed vulnerable. This may sound bad, but there are still an estimated 75,000 speakers of the traditional language.

Compare this to Irish Gaelic (44,000) and it looks healthy. Some remote communities and countries have languages or dialects on the verge of extinction with just a handful of speakers alive. UNESCO are actively involved in preserving these rare dialects before they die out but they probably wouldn't want to call on me for help. I have always struggled with any language other than English. German lessons at school terrified me, and I can still remember trying to get through lessons by avoiding eye contact with the teacher, Mrs. Fleckney. Knots would form deep in my stomach whenever she asked students to read aloud from a passage. Would she pick me? My eyes would stay locked onto the scratched wooden desk, memorising the etchings of the Duran Duran fan that had previously carved their infatuation deep into the stained pine.

After consultation with my form teacher, she advised me that map reading, conversing with strangers, and daydreaming were my finest qualities; maybe she was right.

Our visit to Wales was brief. One moment we were passing signs in dual languages, and then, without any warning, we were back in England and the added attraction of reading Gaelic had vanished. Something else had changed too. The road began to dip and twist as it hugged the contours of the land. Riding became effortless, and we surged forward, invigorated by rolling hills, steep valleys, rich woodlands and tumbling streams that emerged dreamlike from ahead. This was a part of England I had never experienced before, and the next few hours were a delight.

We had entered the Wye Valley, officially declared as an Area of Outstanding Natural Beauty (AONB). These areas are designated by the Government in a concerted effort to preserve and enhance the special qualities of the finest natural landscapes in the United Kingdom. According to the AONB, to gain such an accolade and earn the appropriate protection, these areas must be deemed to possess a "landscape whose distinctive character and natural beauty (are) so precious that it is in the nation's interest to safeguard them."

It is also said that the poet, William Wordsworth, fell in love with the Wye Valley's "steep woods, lofty cliffs and pastoral landscape." It is not only writers that have become smitten with the area. The romanticist painter, JMW Turner, helped immortalise the landscape through his oil and watercolour paintings, and his accomplished collections are still on display at prominent galleries, including the Tate, one hundred and fifty years after his death.

At the heart of the valley, you will discover the Wye River, the first waterway in Britain to be designated a site of Special Scientific Interest along its entire length. We were now riding parallel with the river, although the bitumen road was unable to emulate the natural curves of the water as it cut through dense woodland and meadows.

The sun-dappled road was full of surprises. In places, sharp bends offered a chance to glimpse the sparkling water between gaps in the trees. Sweeping bends were taken at speed, and short, straight stretches offered the chance to embrace the sun on our backs. Surprisingly, very few vehicles overtook us. It seemed, somehow, that we had the road to ourselves, and by the time we reached Hereford, we were elated.

Alan had been correct about the animal pub name. The riders that we had met on the bridge were located in a pub called the Spreadeagle Inn, and we soon joined them. As it turned out, there wasn't a clear winner when it came to their weakest rider. After a few drinks and mild interrogation, it transpired that they all took turns at the front, rarely broke spokes and rode similar types of bikes. On most evenings they were tucked up in bed by 8.30pm, and after only a few days in the saddle, I could understand why.

When Alan mentioned that we normally attempted a pub-crawl at the end of each ride, one of the lads scoffed at his words. But our drinking wasn't bravado; it was social. In each public house we would seek conversation with landlords, chefs, waitresses, travellers and locals. To cycle all day, then crash out in bed after dinner, was not what we wanted.

Maybe years of shift work had conditioned our bodies to staying up late. Maybe we were just different to them. There is no right or wrong way to become an end-to-ender. As long as you enjoy the experience, it doesn't matter whether you are in bed with a cocoa by sunset or tempted by bright lights and music. It was clear that our two groups were very different. They retired for an early night, while we went in search of a bed and breakfast. I doubted we would ever meet them again.

That night, Alan penned a poem by torchlight and presented it to us during breakfast. It read:

We left the B&B just after nine
Magoo said the hill was a steady incline
But the ride turned into a major task
By the halfway point, we were on oxygen masks
Near the top, we began to slow
As the air went cold and it started to snow

11

Day 5: Road to Nowhere

"For true success ask yourself these four questions: Why? Why not? Why not me? Why not now?"
— James Allen

Hereford to Shrewsbury (53 miles)

I watched the dragonfly as it hovered over the garden pond, catching the faint sound of its beating wings as it drifted on the warm breeze. I turned my face to capture the sunlight, sat down on the doorstep, and clasped the warm tea mug towards my chest. It had been a relaxing morning because the day ahead would be an easy one, according to Nick.

He had ridden to Shrewsbury years before and described our day's ride as a walk in the park. This troubled me a little, as nothing had been easy so far, and despite the ambience, I was unsettled.

After four days in the saddle, my personal undercarriage was suffering from chaffing, and no amount of lather in the shower could ease the pain. On our return to the accommodation the previous night, I could no longer mask the agony and eased off my shorts to show the lads. Nick turned away and told me to "man up", but Alan studied the enflamed rashes and mentioned that he had just the remedy.

My thigh muscles were also in trouble, and I had been massaging deep heat cream to ease the tension. They were tender to touch, causing me to walk in a robotic fashion each time I sat up from a chair. I found myself lying on the bed, unwilling to move, and in need of help. As I stared blankly at the ceiling, Alan passed me a tube of lanolin and instructed me to liberally bathe my nether regions with the moisturising cream.

The lads discreetly went in search of a TV room, and I lay alone on the bed. With my eyes closed, I reached out for the lanolin and smeared it lavishly across the enflamed areas. I knew that within a few minutes the cooling effect would calm the redness, and I sunk my head into the pillow in readiness.

But instead of ice I got fire! My crotch was burning and I opened my eyes in disbelief to stare at the nearest tube. It was a squashed tube of Deep Heat. The lanolin lay untouched on the floor where it had rolled. The lads returned half an hour later to find me in the shower, blitzing my lower body with cold water. Eventually I clambered out, limped into bed, requested an ice pack, and rolled away whimpering.

The restless night had left me edgy and the frugal rations dished out for breakfast tempted me to seek time on my own outside. So for now, it was just the dragonfly, the rising sun, and a cottage garden filled with sweet smelling perennials. Gradually, the solitude of the garden lifted my spirits, and as Alan and Nick appeared by the door, I glanced up in anticipation.

'Look, I'm sorry about last night but my gonads were on fire,' I heard myself blurt out. Alan smiled and said, 'At least you have an ailment now, to go along with my dodgy knee and Nick's aching back.'

The three of us set off under a clear sky, with the promise of an easy day and a mid-morning breakfast to make up for the meager provisions offered earlier. But Nick's promise of a relaxing morning got off to a bad start. It might have gone OK, if the plan to stop for bacon and egg sandwiches had been adhered to, but by the time I noticed the café, partly hidden behind a row of trees, they were too far ahead. I shouted their names, but the only living thing that took notice was a herd of sheep in an adjacent field, one of which bleated a reply.

It was a lonely morning. I could have pulled over and devoured a toasted sandwich, but although my stomach rumbled, I craved their banter more than the food. Ten miles later I reached them. They had stopped by the side of the road and Nick was studying his map. As I collapsed onto the ground I heard him mutter, 'Now that is weird! According to the map, there should be an eatery around here somewhere.'

From deep in my stomach, I began to laugh. At first it was a chuckle, but very soon, tears appeared as I rolled around the grass in delusional happiness. Why was I so joyful? My thighs were burning, my stomach grumbled, and I had been wallowing in self-pity for the last hour. But the sun was shining, I was with two friends, and unbeknown to Nick he was riding once again with two broken spokes. Why I found this amusing, I don't know. I think it was because it happened to him so often, and he never complained about repairing them. In fact, he rarely moaned about anything (except youth hostels).

Each morning I was the last to leave and often kept them waiting, while I fiddled with bungee straps and took last minute photos to remind me of the places we would never revisit. They would patiently wait and smile as I manhandled the panniers into position and, before leaving, go in search of the resident pet to say goodbye.

I was fairly clueless on basic bike maintenance, and once again, Nick never complained about helping me and happily squirted oil and tightened bolts to keep the Donegal Flyer limping along. I had only broken two spokes in the trip so far, which Nick fixed for me, and since then, it had become a daily task on his own machine.

Shrewsbury proved to be a delightful country town, complete with rows of timber-framed listed buildings that ordained the medieval streets. It looked to be a place of residence for traders, artisans, historians and merchants. We made our way to the centre, over a wide bridge spanning the River Severn. By the river's edge, families picnicked on the grass, while children played hide and seek in low hanging branches of weeping willows.

Accommodation was difficult to find, as we had been drawn towards the medieval part of town and now found ourselves riding along cobbled backstreets in search of a room for the night. The names of the lanes were enchanting and included foreboding places such as Gullet Passage and Grope Lane. One shop window advertised ghost tours, and on a dark night, there was no doubt that the ancient cobbled streets, dead-end alleys, overhanging buildings, and ancient churches would fire the imagination.

When we eventually found a vacant sign for accommodation, the owner explained, 'You'll have to share a room including a double bed for two of you. The town is very busy at the moment.' He chuckled softly, and while handing over the key he jested, 'I hope you all get on.'

He didn't explain why the town was so busy and we didn't have the energy to ask.

If there was a downside to the daily mileage, it was the local attractions we were too tired or too time-poor to experience. Shrewsbury is close to the world's first arch bridge, made from iron and opened in 1781. It is still standing today and is a place that attracts thousands of visitors per year, but despite its close proximity, it was a bridge too far.

By the time we had showered and changed, our bodies craved fuel, not nostalgia. I had already taken up a notch on my belt, and although we attempted a pub-crawl each evening, they were rarely riotous affairs due to many factors including fatigue, location, and the day of the week.

I am not boasting about our alcohol intake. This was our summer holiday, and many British holidaymakers would be consuming far more during their two-week excursions to the sun. The difference was that we earned our beers by cycling approximately 70 miles each day and consumed water by the gallon while on the road.

Our cramped room was in the attic, with an angled ceiling that caused me little bother but caused Alan and Nick to stoop slightly as they walked towards the bathroom. It had a single bed adjacent to a porthole window, a double bed below a skylight, and a blow up mattress underneath (to be pulled out in case of marital bust ups, I imagined).

Nick dropped his panniers onto the wooden floor, dived onto the single bed, and declared, 'That's me sorted then.'

Alan and I completed a similar manoeuvre at precisely the same moment as each other and landed side-by-side on the double bed, laughing as our eyes stared through the open skylight. Far in the distance, the distinctive trail of an airplane split the sky into two. At the front of the trail, the plane glistened, then vanished behind a passing cloud.

My back eased into the gentle mattress, and already I could imagine lying outstretched after a cool shower, rubbing lanolin cream into my enflamed areas as late night TV illuminated the room.

The problem was Alan. I needed him out of the bed. I was guessing that he was thinking the same thing too, and as I stretched my legs, he asked, 'Well, Ali. How about a game of Trivial Pursuit? The winner takes all.'

I declare now that I cheated. Can you blame me? I needed this more than him. I hadn't set out to lie and deceive, but sometimes, desperate times require desperate acts. Within minutes, the game was over.

After answering my final question out of the six on the card, I had gained four points. Alan was on three points and needed one more to go for the tiebreak. I shouldn't have been surprised that he knew the whereabouts of the Nazca Lines and the resident of 221B Baker Street. And I definitely knew that he would successfully answer the musical question: *Can you name the first ever record played on Radio 1?*

As he hummed *Flowers in the Rain,* I stared at the card in front of me and read his final question. Everyone knows that art and literature questions in Trivial Pursuit are notoriously difficult. Well, they always have been for me. While at school, art and German lessons were my downfall, and I was hoping they were also Alan's Achilles heel. If he got it correct, it would go down to a tiebreak, overseen by Nick, who was too absorbed in the TV weather report to take any notice of the tension now mounting in the adjacent bed.

I have never been any good at tiebreaks and knew what would happen. My childhood stutter would break out while my mind screamed out the answer. Alan, on the other hand, was faster on the draw and would be sure to win the tiebreak. Therefore, he just had to lose on this question.

And so it was on that late summer evening, my eyes fell onto the card, and my heart missed a beat as I read one of the simplest art and literature questions ever written for Trivial Pursuit: *Who painted the Mona Lisa?* I couldn't believe it. Had Nick also packed junior Trivial Pursuit? I reread it; the same question stared back at me.

Alan's eyebrows twitched in anticipation, and I knew he would know the answer. In a desperate attempt to gather my thoughts and claw back time, I dropped the card on the floor. As I knelt to pick it up, I noticed a framed painting on the wall. It was a cheap print, depicting a young boy, lying on the grass, absorbed in a book. The book cover was bright red and distinctively had the word *Dream* in the title.

As I read the card, I turned to Alan and asked, 'Which Russian author wrote the book, *Boyhood Dreams*?'

There was a moment of silence as he contemplated the question, and then he grinned widely and replied, 'Well, I guess that's me on the blow-up bed tonight then. I have no idea, but I'll take a guess.' He pondered for a few moments, then held up a finger and replied, 'Could it be something like Ivan Von Blitzenburg?'

I feigned a chuckle at such a valid but improbable reply, but instantly realised that my knowledge of Russian names was extremely limited and I urgently required a fictional answer. As I shook my head in reply, my mind raced with potential names. The first one in my thoughts was Lech Walesa. But wasn't he the Polish electrician that helped form the Soviet Bloc's first independent trade union movement?

I kept shaking my head and stalled further by standing up and stretching.

'So who is it?' he asked.

'Oh, you would never guess,' I exclaimed as my mind scrambled with suitable answers. What was the name of the Russian president with the birthmark? The one who fought against Ronald Reagan in the

Frankie Goes to Hollywood video? I could see the two of them, sumo wrestling, while the band sang, *We're Two Tribes Going to War.*

The thought vanished, and I returned to reality with Alan staring at me from the bed, waiting for an answer.

Then it came to me in a flash. Mikhail Gorbachev! That was his name.

'Well, Alan, you were nearly correct!' I declared loudly, then stuffed the card deep into the pack, dived onto the other side of the bed, and said, 'It was Ivan Lech Gorbachev.'

'I was close then. Was he related to Mikhail Gorbachev?'

'Probably,' I mumbled and then decided to change the subject as soon as possible and asked Nick for a weather report.

12

Day 6: Day Tripper

"The Beatles saved the world from boredom."
— **George Harrison**

Shrewsbury to Southport (84 miles)

I awoke, like most days, to the sound of Alan whistling. He was normally the first to rise, and with very little effort, would prepare for our departure. On numerous mornings I would find Nick in the front garden with his bike upside down, while he twiddled with gears, levers and spokes before his first cup of tea. Sometimes he would take pity on the Donegal Flyer and I would wake to find him oiling the chain or adjusting sprockets. By now, the borrowed panniers were slowly deteriorating and were held together by safety pins and bungee ropes.

After breakfast, both men waited patiently, as they had done on every other day, while I adjusted the fixings in an attempt to make the lumpy saddlebag as even as possible. We waved goodbye, and with a sixth sense located the ring-road and found ourselves on the road north. After yesterday's excitement, we were strangely subdued, and for the first few miles, there was little chitchat as we kept close to the verge once more.

I had taken a look at the map before our departure and knew that this road headed directly north with few deviations, so in that sense it was very satisfying. In all journeys there must be days when nothing much happens, except you tick off a small part of your ultimate destination. The sun was hidden behind a band of low cloud, and the grey day seemed to ebb my spirit. I felt lethargic and listless and rode without any passion, falling further behind with each mile.

In my estimation, we were about 50 miles north-west of Birmingham. But we were a world away from the spaghetti junction

65

road system that has confused drivers for generations. The main road we were on cut directly through farmland, and we passed fields filled with cows, their black and white spots contrasting against the velvet greens of the lush grass. Some cows were so close to the hedgerow that we could see their eyes as we sped past. Every so often they would startle and start small stampedes as they ran across their meadow. But mostly they were lethargic, with their heads hung low as they munched and mooed.

Other fields were devoid of cattle, with large tracts of ripened wheat, rippling in the cool wind. We zipped through villages, but I took little notice of their names. Most had pubs, some had thatched cottages, a few had village greens, and others had duck ponds. From time to time, we stopped at village shops to top up on provisions. These are the lifelines of many communities, and each shop window did their best to promote local activities or events.

In one window, I read, "*Village fete, Sunday at 10:00 with a bouncy castle for the kids. All welcome.*" Next to that: "*Share trading for beginners. Call Pete for more information.*" In the corner was another: "*Sheep manure — two pounds a bag. See inside for details.*" My favourite was a faded sticker that said, "*Lose weight in four weeks or your money back. Guaranteed results.*"

My personal suggestion for losing weight is somewhat different. Rather than pay thousands of pounds on gym memberships or supplements, spend the money on a trip to Peru. You can trek the Inca Trail for the same cost, lose weight, and have an adventure at the same time. It's far more fun than Weight Watchers. I once read that the average gym membership for a year can cost an entire month's salary, and the drop off rates can be outrageous when New Year's resolutions fade into obscurity.

I know that Peruvian adventure trips are not for everyone, but I hope you get my point. We had been losing weight all week, and for the first time in years, I could see the faint outline of my ribs. I didn't necessarily see this as a good thing, but it seemed that no matter what fuel I fed my body, it was rapidly consumed.

It was clearly a day for thinking, not talking. With Nick and Alan far ahead, my mind raced with thoughts about what this adventure was all about. Yes, we were raising money for charity and also getting fit while undertaking an adventure. But there was something more. For me, anyway. I wanted to complete something worthwhile.

A few years earlier, I attempted to climb to the top of Mount Kilimanjaro in Tanzania and had failed to make it to the summit. I had flown to Africa some weeks earlier with my friend, Owen, and during an overland safari had camped in the Serengeti National Park with only a thin tent separating us from a pride of lions. During the safari, I was struck down with flu, and on the day we commenced the trek in Tanzania, I was still not feeling 100%.

Together with my brother David, who had flown in from London with another friend, Paul, we trekked up the popular Marangu route, staying in huts along the way. For four days, I managed to keep up, although my skull pounded and breathing became harder with each tentative step.

On the day of our summit attempt, I was woken, groggy, just after midnight by our guide, and so began our trek to the top. Six hours later, Owen and I were vomiting into a crater, while Dave and Paul trekked the final steps to the peak.

On our return to England, I watched the homemade video, including the agonising part where my brother and his friend took the video recorder from my shaking hands, and with apparent ease, trekked a few minutes more to the summit. The recording, with them standing proudly on the roof of Africa, shows two fit men, rugged up against the bitter cold, laughing and waving to the camera. At that exact same moment, Owen and I were being escorted down the mountain, close to suffering acute mountain sickness.

Mum would have seen my trek as a victory, but she was no longer alive to congratulate my efforts. How I would love to stop at a phone box now and call her up. To explain where I was, to share my cycling exploits, and to hear her infectious laugh. Now, as I cycled on alone, I hoped she was with me.

Mum left Ireland in her twenties in search of work, and like thousands of others, moved to England. She then got married, had three children, divorced then remarried (this is when Matthew and I came along), and then she divorced again. Many of my uncles and aunties had also moved from Ireland in search of a new life, but instead of England, they had chosen Miami or New York.

I grew up in a council house in an industrial town called Luton. When mum passed away, I was 24 and had just left home to live with a girlfriend. We were struggling to pay the mortgage due to spiralling interest rates, and the emotional turmoil of losing my Mum had sent the relationship to the edge. It was evident that the ending would not be happy.

When Mum died, the American side of our family flew over for the funeral. So too did the Irish, but the Americans arrived a few days early, and within 24 hours, I could sense they were restless. They landed on our doorstep by taxi from Heathrow, and no amount of tea could disguise their unease. Maybe it was mourning, or just because they were staying in a council house in an industrial English town.

My auntie was a colourful character, unafraid to air her thoughts. To ward off the spring chill she wore fur-lined jackets and when she spoke, it was in a slow drawl. One morning, she cornered me in the lounge room and asked, 'So Alistair, what University did you attend?'

I stared at her for a few seconds and answered, 'I didn't. None of us in the family did.'

'How many properties do you want to own?'

'Well I bought one last year with my girlfriend. But house prices are dropping sharply and the mortgage is crippling. I think we're about to split up.'

She reached out to take hold of my hand and squeezed it softly. In a gentle voice, she then asked, 'What are your ambitions, Alistair? Your mum has passed away, God bless her soul, and your dad lives in a small house. Where will you live if you can't pay the mortgage?'

I didn't have any plans, or have a clue where to live, and stared back blankly for a few seconds, my eyes welling with shame and grief.

They decided to fly to Ireland until nearer to the funeral. As the taxi pulled away, my auntie called out, 'See you, honey. You take care. We'll be back on the morning of the funeral. Have a think about keeping your house. It's a great investment for the future!'

While they were gone, Matthew and I blitzed every room of mum's house. Maybe it was our way of dealing with the bereavement, but within a few hours, we had a motto. Use it or lose it. We filled a skip, donated the best contents of Mum's wardrobe to a local charity, and along with other family members, cleaned the house from top to bottom.

On the morning of the funeral, the house was pristine. Family and friends filled every downstairs room, and the kettle was constantly refilled. It was nearly time for the hearse to arrive, but the Americans were running late due to flight delays. When they appeared, there was a frenzy of activity as they bundled out of the taxi and ran upstairs. As I prepared tea, I heard a yell from one of the bedrooms. It was the slow drawl of my auntie.

'Matthew, before we left for Ireland, we put all our clothes in your Mum's wardrobe. Your Uncle had a suit made especially for the funeral. Have you seen them?'

There soon followed a frantic car journey to the charity shop.

Matthew started at one end with my uncle, I commenced at the opposite end with my auntie, and we met in the middle. We managed to locate some of their clothes, but according to the shopkeeper, some items were snapped up within minutes of being put on the shelf. On a positive note, it was nice to see colourful garments worn by the congregation, rather than grey or black, but it took a few years for the Americans to forgive us!

The daydream broke as Alan and Nick came into view. They had stopped to check on my whereabouts and could sense that I was quiet.

'Are you ok?' Alan asked.

'Yes,' I replied. 'Sometimes it gets lonely at the back. I was lost in my thoughts for a while. You know me. Just thinking too deep.' He knew it was about Mum. He punched me playfully on the shoulder and whispered, 'She'd be proud, mate.'

Our next destination was Chester, where friends of mine lived. I arranged the meeting a few weeks earlier and was keen to meet with Martin and Michelle. Nick's map revealed that Chester was an easy day's cycle, and with a brisk wind at our back, we hurtled along the main road. At times I was able to slipstream behind them, and mile after mile swept past in relative ease. Just after lunch, as we settled back into the ride, Alan broke away from the pack without any warning and sped into the distance. Three miles later, we passed him. He was standing underneath the *Welcome to Chester* sign and got high fives as we passed by at speed.

With miles tumbling quickly and the day still relatively young, Nick convinced me that we should keep moving. Birkenhead was another milestone, and we could always get a train back to Chester to see my friends in the evening. I knew that he was right. It was too early in the day to stop, but I sensed that the chance of a reunion was slipping away.

My thoughts were confirmed once we reached Liverpool and threaded our way through the road system until we reached the banks of the River Mersey. Standing in the ticket queue was the group of four that we met on the Severn Bridge. The red haired girl waved and called us over.

'Wow, didn't expect to see you again,' she chirped.

Alan smiled and replied, 'Yes, still hanging in there. How about you?'

One of the lads retorted, 'Yeah, well. We've just been taking it easy really. It's not that hard.'

The girl laughed and said, 'Who are you trying to kid? You've been moaning all week about your groin aching.'

With that, he scurried away, and I went in search of a photo opportunity. On my return, Nick was holding something for me. It was a one-way ticket for a ferry across the Mersey. Martin and Michelle would have to wait until my next visit to Chester.

The ferry broke from shore, and in true Liverpudlian spirit, we crossed the oily waters, listening to the retro sounds of *Gerry and the Pacemakers* singing *Ferry Cross the Mersey.*

The far side of the river was dominated by an imposing building, thirteen floors high with two clock towers strutting out from either end. The Royal Liver Building was once the tallest structure in Europe, and with a prime riverside location, still manages to invoke a feeling of grandeur. Perched on top of the clock towers are two mythical creatures known as the Liver Birds. They stand 18 feet high and were designed by a German woodcarver called Carl Bernard Bartels, who moved to England in the early twentieth century. His accomplishment was not enough to save him from imprisonment in an internment camp on the Isle of Wight during World War I, although he was allowed back into the country after peace was declared.

One of the birds faces the river, while the other looks over the city. Both have a sprig of seaweed in their beaks. Legend says that the city will fall or become flooded if ever the birds fly away. The Liver Bird symbols date back for hundreds of years, and such is their esteem that images of these creatures are found on the Liverpool coat of arms, on numerous placards throughout the city, and on Liverpool Football Club's logo.

As we crossed the Mersey, I attempted to make conversation with the group of four. The women were bubbly and chatty, but the young men were reserved and offered little contribution. As the boat pulled up at the quayside, they all headed for the ring-road towards an unknown destination, and we set off in search of the Beatles.

The city centre was a typical mixture of budget stores, takeaway franchises, banks, travel agents, one-way streets, tin-shakers, cafés, and shoppers. Rain clouds threatened, and most people scampered rather than browsed, so it was with relief that we caught the attention of a pedestrian who stopped abruptly as we called out, 'Excuse me, but we're looking for the Beatles.'

The man was in his mid-thirties and wore a striped tracksuit top and matching bottoms. His receding curls were in need of a wash, but his green eyes were sharp, and as he came closer, he momentarily stared at Nick's Lycra shorts and said, 'Isn't everyone these days? By the way, nice outfit, mate.' Then, after a momentary pause, he announced, 'You're thirty years too late, lads. The Beatles are over. George is dead, and the rest are living in exotic places like Monte Carlo, New York, or the Mull of Kintyre.'

'What about where they played? Is the Cavern nearby?' Alan asked.

'Do you mean the original one or the replacement one?'

'The original, of course,' I replied.

'You're out of luck there too. You know what the city council did to the place where the greatest pop band in the world was discovered? And where bands like The Who, The Rolling Stones and The Yardbirds played some of their first gigs?'

'This isn't going to have a happy ending,' Alan chortled.

'They knocked it down because it was in the way of a friggin' underground railway. And then it became a car park. But here's the good bit. They eventually decided they'd made a huge mistake, somehow found the original bricks, and rebuilt it as near as possible to the same spot.'

'So there is a Cavern then? I asked.

'Well it's still called the Cavern. But it's not exactly the same, is it? Even though Paul came back and played there. I tell you what, though, you can visit the house that McCartney grew up in. I've heard it's still intact; I shagged his second cousin once.'

We ignored this last remark, and Nick asked, 'What about Penny Lane? Is that nearby?'

'Oh, they tore that bus stop down years ago,' he replied quickly, 'like most of the memorable parts of Liverpool.'

As he talked, his arms gyrated like a clockwork robot, and with each sentence, the tone of his speech inched higher.

Without a pause for breath he asked, 'Are you southerners? Softies, hey. Blur and all that nonsense! Have you heard of decent bands like Cast? Probably not.'

Alan interrupted, 'Actually, I have their new album…'

'Well, lads, I've got business to attend to. I can't stand here all day talking with bike riders.'

Then he swiveled 90 degrees on his training shoes, puffed his chest, and strolled towards a nearby pub.

We decided to leave the visit to Paul McCartney's house, fearing that it might have been turned into a McDonald's eatery and decided instead to head to the seaside town of Southport. I found out later that

Paul's house is in mint condition, under the effective management of the National Trust.

Hugging the west coast of England, Southport is essentially a town built for tourism, and although the ease and appeal of budget flights to faraway shores has impacted trade, it remains a sought after location, especially during weekends. We rode towards the centre, passing numerous signs for the pier, and contemplated stopping in one of the many tearooms. A bus-stop placard displayed upcoming events, including an airshow, a food and wine festival, and an evening of jazz.

Clearly, Southport was worthy of more of our time, but after finding suitable accommodation, our only thought was for hot food. With weary legs, we declined all thoughts of exploring a nearby cappuccino strip — lined with restaurants, wine bars and boutique shops — and settled instead for a pub called The Coronation, nestled between a betting shop and a jeweller. The brick exterior was decorated with hanging baskets, ablaze with fresh flowers, and the blackboard promised fine ales, a warm welcome and home-cooked meals.

The clientele consisted of diners, pool players, courting couples, and small groups of patrons enjoying an evening drink. All in all, a perfect local pub, and within moments of entering, we found a vacant table and waited while Alan studied the extensive beer menu.

While chatting about our day, a voice from nearby called out, 'Backpackers, I presume.'

It came from a man who was sitting alone near the bar. He was dressed casually in shorts, shirt and sandals, and smiled warmly, his teeth white against a bushy beard. His tousled hair was losing its battle with grey, and his eyes were partially hidden behind a narrow pair of reading glasses.

'Were you talking to us?' Alan asked.

'Oh yes,' he replied cheerfully and then added, 'I enjoy watching strangers and try to work out their profession and leisure pursuits. I would say that you are school teachers... on a bird-watching holiday.'

'Do you get much wildlife in Southport?' I asked.

'Why, yes! The estuary is a world-renowned bird sanctuary,' he announced eagerly.

'I'm sorry, but we don't bird watch and none of us teach,' Nick explained with a chuckle.

'More importantly, what do you do for a living?' Alan asked.

In a low voice, he replied, 'Ah, my friend, you will have to guess.'

And so began a short game with a friendly man, whom we soon

discovered was called Jim. His attire convinced Nick that he was a builder enjoying an after work drink. He showed us the palms of his hands, tutted disapprovingly, and went back to his crossword. I took a stab at an English teacher, which produced a raised eyebrow and a sly smile as he supped his ale and announced, 'Getting warmer.'

After a few more attempts, Alan guessed correctly. He was a retired lecturer, and without too much prompting, we soon found out that his main passion in life was brass rubbing. When not partaking in his favourite hobby, he was likely to be found at the pub, attempting crosswords, joining quiz teams and talking to strangers.

We shared a round of drinks, and he talked about the regulars, adding names to the conversation as if we knew them well. We then gave a brief summary of our adventures so far. He was silent for a second, then took a slurp of ale and replied, 'I envy your zest for life, lads. I really do. You should feel proud of your adventures. Are you going to walk to the end of the pier before you leave in the morning?'

The pier hadn't entered my thoughts since passing the signposts hours earlier, but Jim was eager to promote its merits. 'It's the second longest in Great Britain and they serve tea at the end. I once rubbed a brass plaque by the entrance. It's a bracing walk, far out to sea, I can tell you.'

I felt a stab of remorse, as I knew that the likelihood of exploring the pier was low. We should have embraced the opportunity, and deep down I wanted to drag myself out of bed to take a dawn walk out to sea. But right now, I was fighting waves of fatigue, and my body was craving carbohydrates.

Food was on everyone's minds. A toasted sandwich arrived for Jim, and we stirred to life, prompted by his recommendation for an Italian restaurant a few streets away. At the doorway, we bade him farewell and stepped onto the darkened street.

Jim had made a good suggestion, and after devouring the house special, I felt my body sliding lower on the plush seats. As if by magic, a bottle of red wine appeared on our table, and Nick led the way in a series of toasts as we wallowed in the glow of another successful day on the road.

Upon leaving the restaurant, we were instantly greeted by a cool wind buffering down the narrow street from the direction of the sea. The sudden drop in temperature invigorated Alan and Nick, and they marched across the road towards the nearest bright lights. I stopped at the curbside, unable and unwilling to follow. My legs felt hollow and a faint sweat trickled down my brow. I called out, 'That's me. I'm done for the night,' and without waiting to get persuaded to join them, plodded through the back streets in search of my bed.

I woke hours later, forced from a dream by a consistent tapping from afar. But unable to hear it again, I closed my eyes once more and turned towards the wall, wrapping the duvet snugly around my torso. Just as I felt myself drifting back to sleep, the tapping returned. It was coming from the window, and each rap seemed louder than the last.

Was it my imagination or could I hear voices, straining to be heard from faraway? I snapped into consciousness, drew back the curtains, opened the window, and peered outside. Swaying in the hazy glow of a streetlamp were two silhouettes, and as I popped my head into view, one of them called in a hushed voice, 'You missed a great night, Ali.'

I suppressed laughter and hissed, 'Shhh. I take it that you need a key?'

The next voice that carried to my window was far too loud for such a late hour. It resonated across the rooftops, and between slurs, could be deciphered as, 'Yes, please. It's bloody freezing. Can you throw one down?'

A shaft of light flooded the pavement as the front door flung open and they were hastily ushered inside. As they sagged onto their beds, Alan slurred, 'I don't think we'll be getting any special marmalade in the morning.' He then rolled over and within seconds was snoring gently.

I woke to the sound of whistling coming from the bathroom and turned my head to look at the clock. They had arrived home in the early hours and it was now just after eight. Alan emerged from the shower, grinned and said, 'Well, there's certainly life in Southport after dark.'

During breakfast, he drew a caricature of Jim and announced he would send him a postcard from John O'Groats.

13

Day 7: He Ain't Heavy, He's My Brother

"There's no such thing as bad weather, only unsuitable clothing."
—**Alfred Wainwright**

Southport to Kendal (62 miles)

Apart from Alan scribbling with a pencil, breakfast was a subdued affair. I attempted to break the ice with small talk about how tasty the Cumberland sausages were, but the landlady just clucked her tongue as she placed a teapot onto the table and strode into the kitchen without a word. When she returned, Alan and Nick apologised for forgetting their key and complemented her on the delicious spread.

A faint smile appeared as she said, 'I don't blame you for going out. But please remember your friggin' key next time. Me head is pounding with lack of sleep after you two eedjets woke the whole bloody street.'

Then she asked, 'Where are you going today?'

'Kendal,' Nick replied hoarsely.

'Kendal… bloody Kendal! On bikes? You must be mad.' She pointed at me and said, 'At least *he* had the sense to be home before midnight.'

She stood with her hands on hips and asked, 'Aren't you all married with kids and the like?'

I explained. 'Nick's married. Alan and I are single.'

She tapped the table and whispered, 'A few years ago I'd have been out on the town with you all, but I'm too old now. I'll tell you what. I'll prepare a few bacon sandwiches to help you on your way.'

As we thanked our host and left the dining room, I asked, 'Talking about marriage, where exactly is Karen meeting us?' My panniers were filling with smelly clothes, and I was keen to get fresh supplies. I could have visited a launderette, but there never seemed to be enough time, and I convinced myself a squirt of deodorant into each compartment would suppress the faint smell of sweat permeating from the depths. I was also down to my final pair of clean underpants.

Nick patted me on the back and said, 'Just one more day until we meet the girls. Not sure exactly where yet, but it will be somewhere in bonny Scotland.'

The detour to Southport had diverted us further east than originally planned, but Kendal was still in our sights. With Nick reading the map, we reset our bearings, packed the sandwiches, bode farewell, and set off at a lively pace.

A few miles out of town, Alan broke two spokes and limped to the back of the pack, while Nick diverted us to Preston in search of a bike shop. By mid-morning, we found ourselves in another town centre, and it suddenly struck me that they were all beginning to look similar — traffic lights, traffic wardens, shoppers dressed for rain, coffee shops with steamed up windows, and too many discount stores.

After circumnavigating the back streets in search of a shop, we came to the conclusion that no one in Preston owned a bike. The obvious answer was to ask a local, but after our encounter with the talkative yet strangely unhelpful character in Liverpool, I sensed reluctance. We stopped outside a café, and with rain threatening, people scurried past us, oblivious to our broken spokes.

Then thankfully, Alan spotted an ideal candidate to ask. He wore chinos, leather shoes, and he sported an open necked shirt. He was in his early thirties, with a healthy thatch of auburn hair, and he was searching the crowd for a familiar face.

'Go ask that bloke, Nick,' Alan said. 'I reckon he's waiting for someone, and he looks like a friendly local.'

'Good idea,' said Nick and handed me his bike.

He walked directly towards the waiting man, who turned to face him as he approached. The man smiled warmly, expecting to be asked a question, but Nick skimmed straight past, towards another pedestrian that we hadn't spotted, directly behind.

This other person had a shock of honey blonde hair, receding at the temples, and wore a pair of round framed glasses. He was rummaging through a rubbish bin, and as Nick approached, he turned his head towards him and stood to attention. From our vantage point and to our amusement, they looked to be identical twins, except for their choice of clothes.

Each of Nick's questions was met with nods of approval. At first it looked hopeful, as the man pointed down the street and waved his hands as if to say, 'Go right.' But then suddenly he seemed to change his mind, rigorously scratched an armpit, and pointed towards a nearby alleyway in the opposite direction. As the question and answer session continued, the man continued to nod in an enthusiastic manner, but they didn't seem to be getting anywhere.

Eventually, a passerby discarded something in the bin, which instantly distracted the stranger, who reached inside, pulled out a brown paper bag, and walked away without a backward glance.

During this façade, the man in chinos had been reunited with his lost partner. She emerged from the throng of shoppers, dressed in bright Lycra, pushing a racing bike. After embracing, they smiled at Nick while walking past, then melted into the crowds. As Nick returned, he called out, 'He was a very nice bloke. But not the full shilling if you ask me.'

'Yes, totally agree,' said Alan as we burst into laughter.

As we approached the foothills of the Lake District, the scenery changed with each mile. The Lake District is the most popular national park in Britain, with over 16 million visitors each year. Within its 885 square miles, you will discover England's highest peak (Scafell Pike, 3,210 feet), its wettest inhabited place (Seathwaite, 130 inches of rain per year), and its deepest lake (Wastwater, 258 feet).

The majority of visitors converge on the main towns and popular attractions, but those that take the time and effort to get off the beaten track can still discover a taste of wild Britain. Mountain bikers crave off-road trails, rock climbers cling to craggy summits, and walkers head for the hills in search of solitude and adventure.

During numerous trips to the Lake District, I have lost count of the number of times I've witnessed groups of able-bodied holidaymakers emerge from coaches, queue for an ice cream, and then walk a few hundred steps along a designated footpath to a lookout area. They are so close to the real thing, but never quite experience the magical beauty that is just out of reach. Twenty minutes later they are back on board, heading to another must see location. I often wonder why they do not take that extra step.

The Lake District is not a pristine wilderness and is under constant pressure. Conservationists want to protect the land from encroachment, farmers feel threatened by marauding hill walkers who stray onto on private land, and mining groups continually solicit for new ventures. Some visitors leave more than footprints, and the summer influx pushes the public services to their limit. Each year, inexperienced trekkers attempt dangerous trails, resulting in injuries and, at times, tragedy.

Thousands of miles of public footpaths crisscross the landscape. Some circumnavigate the sixteen lakes, others lead walkers through tranquil valleys. Long distance hikers use these tracks to enjoy the tranquility and ruggedness of trekking across exposed moorland, before scrambling onto exposed mountaintops.

At the age of eighteen, I was persuaded by my brother Dave (owner of the Donegal Flyer) that a walking trip to the Lake District would be a valuable way to spend my summer holiday, rather than a week away with friends to the Mediterranean hotspot of Ibiza. To this day, I cannot remember why he convinced me that a week of hills, rain and real ale would be better than a week of sea, sun and sangria, but I was glad he did.

Together with our friend, Paul, we trekked 70 miles along a route called the Cumbria Way, from Ulverston to Carlise. Along the way, I learnt to navigate, fell in love with the Lake District, and gained an education on the merits of real ale compared to lager.

The bustling market town of Kendal is the unofficial gateway to the Lake District and became our final overnight stop in England. It was also a Friday, and Alan was able to pull one more pristine shirt from his panniers that evening.

If you ask any hill walker what Kendal is famous for, there is a good chance they will mention mint cake. It has been produced in the town for over 140 years and can be purchased in camping shops throughout Britain. In basic terms, the cake is created from a mixture of sugar, glucose, peppermint and water, although the exact formula is a well-guarded secret. For over a century, they have been used as an essential source of energy for those on expeditions. Sir Edmund Hillary's team ate the individual bars during their successful Everest climb in 1953, Ewan McGregor included them in his supplies during his 2004 motorbike trip around the world, and I consumed them during my trek along the Cumbria Way.

After finding accommodation, we showered quickly and set off in earnest towards town. There was a spring in our step, which I put down to the fact that it was a Friday night. It also helped that the clouds had dispersed and the day's ride had been stress free. We started off at Ye Old Fleece Inn, for no other reason than we liked the name of the pub. The exterior was clad in exposed timbers, and hanging above the doorway was a sign declaring that it had been built in 1654.

With over four hundred years' experience serving weary

travellers, our expectations were high and we were not disappointed. After sampling the Lakeland lamb, washed down with Black Sheep Ale, we found a new surge of energy. While Alan deliberated over the next beer selection, Nick and I studied the Friday night clientele. There were a lot of couples, all making small talk, their voices fighting against the melodic sounds of an 80s compilation album. These, we presumed, were weekenders escaping the city for the lakes.

This section of the pub seemed to have attracted all those from out of town, and not once did I hear a barman call out, 'Same as usual is it, Henry?' or something similar. My guess is that the locals congregated in the snug, or public bar, spending time with their own folk until the summer crowds had dispersed.

The diners alongside us were outsiders, just as we were. By the window, a young couple studied an ordnance survey map. Well the man did, but his partner was struggling to stay interested and suppressed tiny yawns each time she sipped her gin and tonic. They were in their early twenties, dressed in hiking gear with two small rucksacks at their feet. Their boots were stained and the woman's calf muscles were splattered with dirt. She was probably in need of a shower after a full day's walk up Scafell Pike but instead looked to be getting a rundown of their next expedition.

Alan returned from the bar and said, 'Here you go, lads, three pints of Jennings.' As he passed around the drinks, he began humming along with the latest song from the compilation collection, and in doing so, caught the attention of a passing staff member. They ambled over, drawn to his soft singing, and asked, 'Like your music, do you?'

Alan nodded and replied, 'Yes, mate. I love all the sounds.'

'You should try the pub next door later. They have a disco every Friday night. It's mainly locals enjoying a dance and a few beers. You lads look like you'll enjoy it.'

An hour later we were seated next door. Here, there were no exposed beams or plaques declaring the age of the pub. The décor was functional, and the only food available was beer nuts or Walkers crisps. But the clientele was friendly and nodded in agreement as we settled around the last available table. Our timing was impeccable. The mobile DJ had crammed his equipment into a tight corner, his speakers decorated with a trail of flashing lights, and as soon as we were seated, he announced, 'Good evening everyone, my name's Crazy Dave. Let's get Kendal dancing.'

A song burst from the speakers, and before the first words were sung, Alan called out, 'Nirvana! Smells Like Teen Spirit.' A split second later, the lyrics confirmed that he was correct.

Throughout the evening, his knowledge of music astounded me. It helped that that the DJ was playing the soundtrack of our lives. Every record that I owned, wished for, or had once loved, pulsated across the packed room. As the evening progressed, the level of intensity increased and we joined the residents of Kendal on the dance floor as they gyrated with abandonment. By midnight it was all over. We thanked Crazy Dave, promised to return to Kendal one day, and stepped into the black night.

While staggering home, the smell of a food van diverted our attention, and very soon we were sitting on a park bench, scoffing shish kebabs.

Between munches, Alan asked, 'So lads, what's your favourite music lyric?'

Nick was lying on the grass, mumbling something about falling stars, so I replied, 'I saw two shooting stars last night. I wished on them but they were only satellites.'

'Yes, New England is a top song,' he replied.

'What about you?' I asked.

'Well on a night like tonight, you can't go past: why pamper life's complexities when the leather runs smooth on the passenger seat.'

And with that, we lifted Nick from the grass and arm in arm, walked along the dotted line of the high street singing *This Charming Man*.

At the garden gate, Nick stopped abruptly and announced, 'Look guys. Tomorrow, I'm meeting Karen. I need a bit of time alone with her, if you know what I mean.' Before we could reply, he stated, 'You'll both like Sam. She's a real character. Loves her music and she's single at the moment.'

'I'm not looking,' Alan declared with a chuckle.

'Neither is she, Alan, but be warned. I have a knack of finding her husbands. I did it once before, and one of you two might be next.'

'Does she know the words to all The Smiths' songs?' Alan asked.

'I don't have a clue, but you can ask her tomorrow when she hands you your new set of clothes.' Then we tiptoed down the corridor, slipped into our beds, and once again I awoke to the sound of whistling as Alan emerged from the shower room, refreshed and eager to depart.

14

Day 8: Sunshine after the Rain

"I'm William Wallace, and the rest of you will be spared. Go back to England and tell them Scotland is free!"
    —William Wallace
        Kendal to Moffat (88 miles)

'Well, this is it, lads. Today is the end of England, and the beginning of a very long hill towards the village of Shap,' Nick informed us over breakfast. The trip was going quickly, and I felt elation and sadness, all in one go. Yes, we were getting nearer to our goal with each broken spoke, but for me, this was a holiday that I didn't want to end.

Undulating roads are common in the heart of the Lake District, but I was surprised at the lack of dips on the road out of Kendal. The lakes, hills and mountains were far to our left, while the terrain north of the town was much flatter than I had envisaged. Indeed, the road to Shap was not going to be a torturous journey of inclines — with fast hills to tear down, followed by torturous recoveries going back up — which had been the case in Cornwall, Devon and also parts of Somerset. The road to Shap was different.

For nine miles it offered no respite. The only way was up. In places, the angle was not too severe, maybe three or four degrees, but in others, the steepness increased to eight or nine degrees, forcing riders to earn every yard gained. Slowly, but methodically, we clawed our way through a steady head wind up the hill. At one point, we would have passed by a marker that is meant to show the halfway point between Land's End to John O'Groats — if such a marker exists, because none of us saw it.

The road carved through meadows of purple heather, and at times, we rode alongside massive electricity pylons and could distinctly hear crackles and hums from the overhead wires. Like giant stick men, they were rooted to the spot, each one planted at precise intervals across the landscape. To my right, they progressively grew smaller, like giant robots on the move, and then disappeared into distant valleys.

The weather was cool, but cotton wool clouds rolled past without a threat. As usual, Alan and Nick were ahead, but not by far. To my left, the land looked untamed. There was no livestock, or crops, and very few farms. The wild grassland spread for miles, with dips and gashes adding texture and colour to the landscape. Further to my left, the faint glimpse of a distant peak tempted me to call out for a diversion. But in reality, like so many other natural attractions we briefly spotted, they were stored in memory, to experience another day.

We spotted a mobile breakfast van, its serving hatch lined with hungry truck drivers, but as we cycled past, the thought of queuing for egg and bacon sandwiches seemed like an unwanted distraction. We had found a rhythm and just kept pumping our legs. It was at this stage that I realised my neck was free from sweat. It helped that the cool air was refreshing, but there was something else happening. I no longer required quotes from *Rocky* films to get me through my pain barriers. My legs continually moved without me willing them to do so. I was programmed now to push down on the pedals in a repetitive manner, regardless of the angle of the hill. My vision was clear, I could take time to appreciate the remote scenery and still had the sharpness to steer sharply when a passing lorry loomed too close. Finally, I was getting fit.

I found myself searching for the names of alluring places we would never visit during this trip. Skelsmergh sounded appealing, but it was two miles away, along a narrow road to our right. Crookdale Beck, somewhere to our left, triggered thoughts of a hamlet with a bubbling brook, where we could stop for a while to bathe our aching feet.

But instead, we kept moving. For a while we cycled parallel with a stream, home to many ducks, and once or twice they became startled by our presence and took flight. Their wings momentarily skimmed the bright water before finding lift, and they flew past our small convoy to resettle further downstream.

Maybe this was Crookdale Beck? But I would never know. I just kept cycling. I rode past a sign for Wet Sleddale and wondered why it had earned such a name. Maybe Wet Sleddale was the second wettest inhabited place in all of England? The signpost for the village came and went, just like all the other signposts, farm tracks, abandoned cars, wooden posts, broken fences and discarded bottles that we glimpsed briefly and forgot immediately.

From nowhere, a dense mist descended, engulfing us. For a short period, we each cycled alone, wrapped in a moist grey blanket. The wind stirred, allowing the sun to peek through, and as the mist vanished, the lads appeared — always ahead and always pedalling.

How different the road to Shap would have been if the gods had been against us. For those that encounter inclement weather, the results can be treacherous. During winter storms, the A6 to Shap can become impassable due to snowdrifts. Even in spring and summer, temperatures are known to drop sharply. Over millennia, rain, sleet, ice and wind have carved the landscape, but these elements have not deterred people from exploring one of the last remaining wilderness areas in England.

For those that prefer camping, or being as close to nature as possible, a bothy is strategically located close to the A6 near Shap. A bothy may sound romantic, but in essence it is a place of refuge, designed to protect visitors from the elements. There are few creature comforts, such as electricity and running water, but you will be grateful for the stout roof and solid walls to shield you from the wind and protect you from wolves.

Only jesting about the wolves. By the sixteenth century, wolves were eradicated in England, however they managed to survive in Scotland until at least 1680, when a Scottish Highland Chief by the name of Sir Ewan Cameron killed the last known one.

Undeclared sightings continued for hundreds of years, up until 1888. By then, it was widely accepted that they had been hunted to extinction. There is talk about re-introducing wolves to Scotland, but until this happens, you have as much chance sighting a haggis running across the moors as you would a wolf.

The bothy near Shap is a small white building. Blink and you will miss it. It was originally designed to house a telephone repeater station, and I'm guessing that in this digital age it is no longer required. Due to its remote location, it has gained a reputation as a unique location to hold full moon parties with live music from travelling musicians creating an exclusive event. While driving a car, you would probably hurtle past the bothy and not give it a second glance. On a wild and windy night, or during a snowstorm, this tiny building might just save your life.

We cycled alongside but saw no signs of travelling musicians or hippies preparing for the next full moon. It resembled an abandoned outhouse — alone and unloved.

Stone walls, constructed from locally sourced material such as granite, segregated the road and adjoining fields. Without the use of cement or grout, these walls are sturdy enough to contain farm-stock and stout enough to withstand the onslaught of high winds that are prevalent throughout the seasons.

On some tight bends, the walls had been replaced by functional, but far less appealing, metal railings that wrapped around each corner. They reminded me of the plastic strips used in Scalextric to ensure toy racing cars didn't career off the high banks and smash into the TV.

The incline eventually tapered, and signs of civilisation appeared once more as farmland gave way to houses. Many were constructed from local stone and looked solid enough to survive a tornado. We passed a school but heard no laughter. The playground was empty. School was out for summer, and I wondered where the locals went for their holidays. Did they ramble across nearby hills and mountains and stay in youth hostels? Or did they head to the bothy for moon parties with lost Germans? My guess is that many would travel far away, in search of Mediterranean climes to warm their bones. Who could blame them? As stunning as the Lake District is, sunshine is never guaranteed, and winters can mean long nights, bleak days and biting wind.

Despite the pub blackboard advertising a roast lamb special, the cool weather dampened our spirits and our appetites. For the first time in days, the possibility of a wholesome lunch was surpassed for a quick snack from the village shop. By the time we reached the outskirts of Carlisle two hours later, the talking had stopped. Nick had pinged two spokes and relegated himself silently to the rear of the pack. Alan declined the chance to speed towards the town entrance, I was no longer interested in sky gazing, and collectively we misjudged the broody clouds as they massed silently around us.

A Burger King outlet appeared in the distance, and without a word, Alan led us to the entrance, just as a clap of thunder shook the darkened sky. Rain came down in angled sheets, driven by a freezing wind, and we scurried for shelter from the pea-sized droplets. Nick decided that the automatic doorway would be a good place to replace the broken spokes, and as customers muttered quietly and stepped over his bike frame, Alan and I went in search of a high carbohydrate takeaway.

I hoped no one was watching while I greedily devoured the Whopper and large fries. My hands had been shaking, not from hypothermia but from over exertion. I was beginning to question our diet for such a trip. When was the last time I had eaten a piece of fruit? I made a mental note to ease off the Mars Bars and stock up on something more natural. It was time to invest in a bag that would sit on the front, similar to the one that Nick had been using.

As the rain cleared, Alan asked, 'Did anyone pack waterproofs?' Nick and I looked at each other and shook our heads as he explained, 'Well, next door is an Army & Navy Store, and as the clouds might be with us all week, I suggest we get some.'

Being an army store, most of the goods for sale were khaki green, and the friendly salesman, who resembled a retired grenadier, proudly showed us the items on offer.

'These are waterproof jackets, similar to the ones used in the Vietnam War. They will repel monsoonal downpours. They're also mosquito proof and will last for years.' We nodded in agreement but balked at the price.

'Do you have anything for sale that's under thirty pounds?' I asked.

His brow furrowed, and he took us to another aisle. 'Well, if you don't mind getting sweaty, these will keep the rain off your back, but they're heavy, and to be truthful, the seams can leak in battle conditions.'

Alan replied, 'Cheers, mate, but we're just after a poncho or something simple.'

'Oh, yes, I used to use ponchos when on patrol in Cyprus back in the day. They are cumbersome with all the kit on your back, but its bloody cold in January I can tell you…'

'These will do,' Nick called out.

He was standing by the bargain bucket and held a poncho in the air. Even from a distance it looked thin, and a slight breeze wafting through the doorway flapped its edges. 'How much for these mate?'

'Well they're five pounds each, and I only have one yellow one left. The rest are green. But they are only designed for light showers, so I…'

Nick called out, 'Great stuff, we'll take three.'

Before leaving the shop, I noticed a rectangle-shaped, waterproof pouch that looked purpose-built for the handlebars of the Donegal flyer. Velcro straps secured it easily, and its first use was to hold the new poncho and two apples from a farm shop next door. The fruit stayed inside for the remainder of the day, but the waterproof was in use before we left Carlisle.

The wind was lively, gusting from the west and bringing with it bursts of sideways rain that bounced off the A6 main road. Not that this seemed to deter the traffic. Cars and lorries whizzed past at the same speeds as before, but this time something was different. We were being nudged into the verge by the gusts and needed to concentrate to keep the bikes in a straight line. At the same time, our bare legs were saturated with spray from passing traffic. As the cold front intensified, a low bank of dark clouds and constant drizzle reduced visibility to the extent that it now resembled a dour winter's day.

Nick had claimed the yellow poncho, and I could see the logic of wearing such a bright colour. The khaki ponchos blended in perfectly with the muted landscape, and I was guessing that some motorists didn't notice Alan or myself until the very last second. More than once, the large wheel of a freight truck passed within inches of my head, and I continually questioned the sanity of attempting the ride in such conditions. Main roads meant the chance of success in under thirteen days, but did they also increase the odds of ending up underneath a truck? There are those that argue that winding roads with blind corners are just as hazardous. At this moment in time, I had my doubts.

I watched helplessly as trucks thundered towards my friends, but they could not hear my screams to pull over. Each time, they survived each encounter and slowly but surely faded from view.

This time, I decided to hunt them down and kept a steady, committed pace until they were back on my radar. Mile after mile I clawed back the gap, but the exertion was taking its toll. As I cycled, the poncho swished around my torso and twitched in front of my face, distracting me from the task of keeping in a straight line while freak gusts continually ripped across the tundra, threatening to cast me into the verge.

A burst of rain tore down from the heavens, each droplet bouncing on the tarmac like ball bearings; I squinted to see the greasy road. As the rain eased, I dropped my guard and lifted my bottom to ease aching buttocks. My timing was impeccable. A gust of wind snatched the edge of the poncho and wrenched it into the air. My arms, which were locked onto the handlebars, were the only thing that stopped it from spiralling into the sky. Totally blind, with an inverted poncho blocking all vision and the thunderous roar of an approaching vehicle, I needed to act fast, and I swerved left towards the safety of the verge.

A removal van passed by, oblivious to my plight as my front wheel bit into soft mud and skidded to an undignified stop. I toppled sideways onto the ground and lay still, listening to the rain, the wind and my heavy breathing as I contemplated giving up for the day. But there was no one to help me up. The only sound was the whooshing of vehicles racing past, the drivers unaware that I was flat on my back only a few yards away.

I stood, wiped mud from my face, and squinted into the distance. Far ahead, disappearing into the gloom, I could just make out the blotchy outline of my compatriots. They too were fighting battles and were oblivious to my Marilyn Monroe escapades. There was nothing to do but get back on, but this time I ensured the bottom of the poncho was secure before venturing onto the main road. As I set off, with the poncho wrapped tightly around the saddle, I retracted to a single goal. I just had to keep the wheels pointing straight and ride steadily. Through the gap in my hood, I could see the immediate path, and I blocked out all thoughts of passing traffic and started out afresh.

The strategy worked, and I quickly found myself cocooned from reality, thinking of nothing but the next pedal revolution. By mid-afternoon, the clouds began to disperse. For the first time that day, I saw blue in the sky, and very soon afterwards passed a sign that read, *"Scotland: 20 miles"*.

Alan and Nick were waiting just ahead and had ordered me a mug of tea and a bacon sandwich from a roadside vendor. 'Well, that was interesting,' Alan declared with a smile.

'Interesting? Insane more like,' I pronounced and without another word devoured the sandwich. Rarely had food tasted so good.

Nick looked relaxed after our dice with death and seemed more interested in his mobile phone. He peeled his eyes from the screen and explained, 'Just read a text from the girls. They left Ampthill about three hours ago and should be in Scotland at about the same time as us.'

His statement struck me as comical. During the time that we had been flirting with danger, changing spokes, dressing like Martians, braving the elements, and losing weight quicker than we could replenish it, the girls had driven 210 miles towards Scotland.

I would never again take for granted the amazing qualities of cars. They whisk you from A to B in air-conditioned, soundproof luxury. Not only that, but drivers get treated to stereo surround sound, coffee cup holders, and head rests.

The most direct route to Scotland via Cumbria is along the M6 motorway, but cyclists are banned — for logical reasons, along with horse drawn carriages and space hoppers — so we detoured through the town of Longtown. Like many border communities, many of its inhabitants live and work across both countries. The Treaty of York established the official border for the two countries in 1237, and in places it follows natural contours, alongside rivers and through valleys. On the east coast, it commences at England's most northerly point, Marshall Meadows Bay, and 96 miles later, ends on the west coast at the fertile waters of Solway Firth.

As Scotland approached, the clouds played cat and mouse with the sunshine, but returned for one final downpour as we neared the border. We were now on a B-road, passing through farms, meadows, and across bubbling streams. The road meandered gently, and in places we rode three astride, but a series of curves forced us into single file for the final stretch of England.

Up ahead, on the right, the first clue for Scotland appeared. It was an imposing brick building, surrounded by manicured grounds, complete with an enticing beer garden. The Gretna Chase Hotel looked very appealing, but our thoughts now were on the border and all eyes were peeled for the Scotland sign.

We traversed a bridge and took little notice of the bubbling stream that cut the meadow into two. It was in fact the River Sark, a tributary of the Solway Firth and a natural boundary between England and Scotland. Just after the bridge, on the left, we could see the signpost for Scotland. I braced myself for a late dash to the border by Alan or Nick, but as pre-arranged, we crossed into our third country in unison, and a rare flicker of sunshine warmed our smiling faces.

For centuries, Scottish and English clans have battled for control of the border territories, and some communities have changed landlords numerous times. For example, the Duke of Gloucester raided Scotland in 1482, and after a skirmish, claimed the town of Berwick. It has remained a part of England ever since. Ironically, it is so close to Scotland that their professional football team is allowed to play in the Scottish football league. It is the only English team to do so, and this decision makes sense when you calculate that the town is closer to Edinburgh than Newcastle. If they were ever transferred into the English league and had to play a town such as Plymouth, it would mean a 1000 mile round trip. What a sour return journey that would be if they lost!

The fierce rivalry between England and Scotland still remains. Although land grabs and skirmishes are now resigned to the history books, international football matches between the countries are still notoriously passionate. In 1872, Scotland played England at Hamilton Crescent, Glasgow. The 0-0 draw assured a rematch, and up until 1989, they played against each other every year (apart from the two world wars) resulting in one of the longest running international fixtures in the world.

If ever you want a party to ignite, invite the Scots or the Irish. Add live music and suitable refreshments and you have a guaranteed recipe for merriment. Scottish fans that travel to see their country play football are known as the Tartan Army, and during the 1970s, each match in London was a sellout, with tens of thousands of Scottish "invading" the capital city.

They came by train, coach, car and plane, although many of course already lived in England, and this was their chance to show allegiance. Games that took place during the summer months saw the capital city awash with tartan. Scots congregated in their thousands at traditional landmarks, including the fountains at Trafalgar Square. The wail of bagpipes competed with slurred catcalls, denouncing England, and renditions of *Up with Bonny Scotland*. International tourists took photos, English fans kept their distance, and the police attempted to quell major drunkenness and disorderly behaviour with swift action. Like a problem child, the Tartan Army was on the whole tolerated, officials knowing that in a few days the capital would return to "normal."

This all changed in 1977. Passions were riding high, with Scotland riding on a wave of euphoria following their successful qualification into the World Cup finals due to take place in Argentina the following year. Their manager, Ally MacLeod, had promised they were going to "really shake them up" (the Argentinians) when they won the World Cup.

Before their departure for South America, the Scottish team played in the British Championships and travelled to Wembley in high spirits. With recent wins and a newfound belief, the euphoria and hype swelled the numbers of the travelling Tartan Army. Out of the 98,103 sellout crowd, 70,000 were estimated to be of Scottish origin. Did I mention that my Dad was born and raised in Scotland? He moved to England in his early twenties in search of work and never lost his accent or his love of Scotland.

On the day of the game, he proudly wore a tartan beret and stashed a crate of beer onto the packed coach. Each window was emblazoned with flags and banners depicting the Scottish national flag, and as I waved goodbye, the bus driver beeped his horn and fifty supporters broke into drunken song. It wasn't even midday.

Later that evening, while enjoying a fish and chip supper in front of the TV, a newsflash interrupted Bruce Forsyth's game show to inform us about a pitch invasion at the stadium. Scotland had won 2-1, and as soon as the final whistle had been blown, thousands of delirious supporters streamed onto the pitch. Players were quickly ushered from the field as ecstatic fans celebrated in wild abandonment.

The TV cameraman captured an impromptu moment as one supporter was hoisted onto a crossbar and, with hands held wide, sung his heart out. A few seconds later, another fan joined him and then another. The crossbar snapped, causing a roar from the crowd as it buckled, sending supporters sprawling onto the grass.

Police scurried onto the pitch, but their minuscule numbers were powerless. When the crowds dispersed, the extent of the damage became evident. The goalposts were snapped, the nets had vanished, and in hundreds of places, the grass had been scalped or ripped, then taken away as souvenirs. Wembley Stadium now resembled a war zone instead of a prestigious sporting arena.

When I awoke the following morning, Dad was pottering in our back garden. I ran down to investigate and discovered a small section of lawn had been replaced with a shoebox size of turf. The new section was a richer green than our lawn, velvety to the touch with specks of white paint along one severed edge.

Mum scolded Dad for ripping up part of the 'perfectly good lawn,' but as word spread throughout the neighborhood, it quickly became a place of legend. Despite my efforts to protect and nurture this rare habitat, it eventually took a pounding. Mum trampled on it while hanging out the washing, the dog sniffed and urinated on it, and every kid in the street wanted to take a penalty kick from it. Within days, our hallowed clump of grass withered and died.

In stark contrast, the meadows surrounding Gretna as I cycled on were ablaze with colour. Dragonflies hovered over clear streams, and sun ripened blackberries flourished among the myriad of wildflowers lining the roadside verges.

We passed a building that claimed to be the last pub in Scotland. Once more we pushed on, past buildings claiming to be the first or the last, depending on which direction you were heading. A brick building, with a large car park and manicured gardens, displayed a banner that claimed thousands of weddings had taken place inside. I wasn't sure if this was a good thing or a bad thing. It sounded like a conveyor belt to me.

Gretna Green's rise in popularity can be linked to Lord Hardwicke's infamous Marriage Act, which came into force in

England in 1754. Its aim was to ensure that couples under the age of 21 years could not be married unless both sets of parents agreed.

The answer for those eager (or desperate) to get married was to elope to Scotland, where the laws were far more relaxed. So relaxed, in fact, that boys as young as 14 could marry girls of just 12. Those that made the trip north, usually under some type of duress, naturally sought the first building in Gretna Green, and with blacksmiths playing a pivotal role in many rural communities, their close proximity to the border triggered an era where "anvil priests" performed swift ceremonies for the price of a few coins or a wee dram of whisky.

It wasn't only blacksmiths that could declare a couple to be man and wife. Due to the obscure regulations at the time, pub landlords, farmers and shopkeepers also carried out ceremonies. The rest, they say, is history, and getting married in the Blacksmith's Shop at Gretna Green is a lucrative business. It is estimated that 5,000 couples tie the knot in the village each year, making it one of the most popular wedding locations in the world.

Signs for the original Blacksmith's Shop were located near every roundabout, and without a thought, we silently followed the arrows. We had been in the village a few minutes and were lost in our own thoughts as we cantered peacefully along the pleasant streets. It was a surprise then to have a car drive alongside and beep its horn, and then turn into the train station car park where it stopped abruptly. I knew at once who it was, and as the doors opened, out stepped Karen and a girl I had never seen before.

The last time I had seen Karen she had been serving fresh pizza and advising Alan and I to pack fresh underpants for Scotland. The girl standing alongside her had to be Sam. She was dressed for the mountains, in a thin fleece and cargo pants and gave a tentative smile. Her hair was longer than Karen's, and the colour of warm amber. As she moved away from the car, the wind tugged gently at her soft curls.

She greeted Nick with an affectionate hug and then smiled sheepishly as Alan and I dismounted to say hello. Nick took the initiative and announced, 'Sam, this is Alan and Ali.'

He then turned his attention to Karen, and they embraced across his handlebars as we stood close by, smiling in admiration at their romantic greeting.

Alan broke the ice and said, 'I'm Alan. Pleased to meet you.'

She smiled brightly and replied, 'Me too. I've heard lots about you both.'

They tentatively exchanged kisses on each cheek, and as they drew apart, he explained, 'This is Ali.'

She giggled and replied, 'Well, I never would have guessed.'

It was a strange feeling, to see someone that you have heard about but never seen. She seemed very assured and greeted me warmly as I shook her hand and leaned forward to kiss her cheeks.

We then fell silent and cast our gaze towards Karen and Nick. They pulled away from their embrace and Karen asked, 'Are you all happy to stay in Moffat tonight? We can drive ahead to find accommodation and can lighten your loads by taking those ghastly, smelly panniers with us.'

No one argued. It was a perfect plan and after a warm embrace from Karen, I dismantled the panniers and prepared to leave. As I stowed the bag in their car, I heard a soft chuckle as Alan made small talk with Sam. As the girls sped off, Nick was eager to pursue at speed, while Alan followed quietly, seemingly lost in thought.

After the euphoria of meeting the girls, the road to Moffat was arduous, despite the idyllic views that should have lifted our spirits. Wildflowers carpeted the verge, and bees continually buzzed, drawn to their sweet scent. Bright butterflies floated on the breeze, and birds of all types swooped overhead.

The drone of faraway tractors resonated across the land as farmers prepared hay for winter, and more than once, cows followed our journey from fields of lush grass. We rode close together and attempted a game of Trivial Pursuit, but constant traffic meant that only one question was answered over a five-mile period, and in frustration, Nick threw the card into a hedge.

Moffat proved to be a charming town, and the girls managed to secure us rooms in a picture postcard residence called Spur Cottage. The proprietors, Jack and Daphne, greeted us at the garden gate like long lost relatives, not strangers staying for just one night. They were a sprightly pair and dashed around with the enthusiasm of youth, despite the fact that they were nearing retirement.

Alan towered over Daphne, and it seemed that she took an instant shine to him. They stood in the doorway, side by side, sharing small jokes and talking about the weather. I thought back to Nick's requests while in his garage, and it looked like we had found the perfect Scottish couple to look after us for the night. With her grey hair, glasses, and floral apron, Daphne perfectly resembled our image of a Scottish farmer's wife, and by the permanent grin on Nick's face, I could tell he was a happy man.

Before we had chance to locate our beds, we were invited inside for tea and scones. The house smelt of freshly cut flowers, and each room was adorned with little knick knacks, which added a sense of character to the stone cottage.

As the day drew to a close, we sat in the back garden to embrace the evening sunshine. Cold beers appeared; Daphne emerged from the kitchen with a plate of nibbles, and together with Jack, joined us for a sundowner. Birds darted from tree to tree, watched closely by the resident cat as we lazed on summer loungers and shared stories about our day.

Armed with fresh underpants and a change of clothes, we joined the girls for a night on the town. After our meal, Alan declared a toast and returned from the bar with a tray of drinks. 'Here we go then, a wee dram of ten-year-old whisky to celebrate our arrival in Scotland,' he announced cheerfully.

We raised our glasses, clinked them together, and collectively sipped the fine malt. As expected, it rasped against my throat and warmed my stomach. I was content, for now, just to try the one, and as Nick ordered another round, I slipped out of the doorway in search of a public telephone.

I called Dad to tell him where I was and to explain how the trip was going. He had been living on his own since a divorce from mum twenty years earlier and still struggled with loneliness. After a few minutes debating the last time I had visited him, he asked, 'Have you been to Pitlochry yet?'

'No, Dad, I don't even know where that is.'

'It's on the west coast. Take a cycle ride over there. It's the prettiest place in Scotland.'

'But we're on the east coast. On the way to Edinburgh.'

There was a pause, and then he said, 'Next time we'll go together and explore the Isle of Skye as well. Good luck, son, and keep off the whisky.'

I would plan a trip to the Isle of Skye with Dad when I returned home. My head was brimming with other plans too, and with a sense of purpose, I went in search of my friends. Over the next few hours, we toured the town, sampling the hot spots and enjoying banter with the locals. Most were keen to share secret spots that shouldn't be missed, but I knew that in the morning we were bound for Edinburgh, with little time to deviate.

During our homeward stroll, we discovered the world's narrowest hotel (according to the plaque on the wall outside) and could not resist having one for the road in the Star Hotel. Considering it was only 20 feet wide and not much longer, the place should have been packed to the rafters, but we found a free corner and made ourselves acquainted with those standing close by. As you can imagine, in such a small space it was standing room only, except for a few stools hugging the bar. Luckily it was beginning to thin out, and after ordering our drinks, the landlord announced last orders.

Nick was in deep discussion with Karen. I turned towards Alan and Sam, but they were in animated conversation. Above the noise of the small but lively crowd, I could hear them talking about music and must see holiday destinations. I left them for a few minutes and perched myself on the nearest barstool, nodding to a man in his mid-twenties, who occupied the adjacent seat. He was dressed in trainers, jeans and a checked shirt, and he had a mop of wavy brown hair.

Like many patrons I had seen that evening, he courted a pint of beer along with a small glass of whisky and took turns sipping them both. 'Nice pub,' I said to break the ice.

'It's a hotel, but I know what you mean,' he replied and turned to face me. We exchanged small talk for a while, and I let slip about the bike ride to John O'Groats and then pointed to Alan and Nick

'Who are the lasses then?' he asked.

'Well, Nick is married to the dark haired girl called Karen, and that's her friend, Samantha. Alan and I met her for the first time today.'

He smiled and said, 'Looks like the big fella is getting to know her pretty well, wee man.'

I followed his gaze and grinned in agreement. Yes, they were getting on very well, I thought.

He began to tell me a story, and I found myself leaning closer, trying hard to grasp the words as they fell quickly from his rambling mouth. His strong accent was difficult to decipher, even for me with a Scottish father. I nodded every so often, hoping to decipher just some of the key words tumbling from his lips, just so I could follow the conversation. But my fatigue and his strong dialect meant the conversation spluttered to an end.

He ordered another drink and kindly purchased one for me. We sat side by side, two strangers sipping malt, watching fellow patrons through the distorted mirror of the optics bar.

The landlord rang a bell, then placed a beermat over the pumps, and started making noises about closing time. My new found friend called out for a final drink, and my head was beginning to spin. I decided to leave him in peace, but he caught my arm and gently tugged me back as I bade him goodnight.

'See you, wee man. Whatdya wanna ride all the way to John O'Groats for, you silly bastard?'

I patted him on the shoulder and announced proudly, "Cause it's there.'

And with George Mallory's words of wisdom, I eased off the stool and ushered the others out of the hotel and into the night air. Back at Spur Cottage, I collapsed into bed, fell into a deep sleep and woke once more to the sound of whistling.

15

Day 9: Tequila Sunrise

"All journeys have secret destinations of which the traveller is unaware."
— **Martin Buber**
Moffat to Edinburgh (52 miles)

It was a bird. I lay for a while, listening to its melodic call from a nearby tree and then tuned into another sound. It was Alan, snoring gently from the other bed.

I rarely whistle in the shower, but for some reason I attempted a rendition of *Danny Boy* that morning. As I waltzed back into the room, invigorated by the power shower, I flung open the curtains to greet the day and caught sight of Alan.

He stared blankly into space, his eyes droopy, and then pulled the covers over his head and turned to face the wall. A loud knocking from next door caught my attention, increasing in tempo with every second as the headboard oscillated through the dividing wall. Within seconds, the noise ceased, replaced by the sound of birdsong once more.

The breakfast table was set for a banquet, decorated with fine china and frilly place mats depicting highland cattle. As we walked in, Daphne asked, 'Good morning, lads and lasses, how was your night?' Before we could answer, she explained, 'I have tattie scones for you to take on the road and a cooked breakfast is on the way. I hope you like mushrooms and black pudding. The eggs are free range, and the bacon is from a local farmer.'

Alan was unusually quiet, and she instinctively offered him two headache tablets then asked if he had been enjoying the local refreshments. He nodded his head in agreement and silently swallowed the pills. At the head of the table, Nick sat happily, his mouth in a permanent grin as he poured tea for Karen.

As we tucked into the food, Daphne departed for the kitchen and

Nick raised a dainty tea cup towards me and said, 'This, Ali, is why I don't do youth hostels!'

He certainly looked like all his needs had been fulfilled, which I felt was more to do with Karen's arrival then the extra serving of black pudding. At the opposite end of the table, Alan requested more orange juice as he tentatively tucked into his eggs. Sam passed him the jug and said, 'You certainly enjoyed those wee drams last night, didn't you?'

He smiled weakly and went in search of the bathroom. Back in our room, he quietly packed his fresh clothes into the panniers, and I watched as they were seamlessly layered into each compartment. It was like he owned a Tardis. On the outside, it was just a black set of waterproof panniers. But at any given moment, he could dig out pressed jeans, crinkle free shirts, and pristine t-shirts.

My ripped panniers were now shapeless and lay lifeless on the bed. Try as I might, each garment sat awkwardly in the uneven folds, and six days' worth of fresh clothes already resembled the inside of a clothes dryer after it had finished its cycle.

It was nearly midday by the time we said farewell to Jack and Daphne, departing with hugs and handshakes and the hope that we would someday meet again. The girls would take the high road and we would take the low road, and the plan was to meet them in John O'Groats. Alan dropped to the back of the pack, staying close to my rear wheel as we huffed and puffed up a series of abrupt hills.

We had dressed for mountains, and very soon, had to stop to remove unwanted layers as sweat condensed on furrowed brows. Alan was still at the rear, silent for a change, which was a little unnerving as I had grown used to his cheeky smile and occasional wit.

The incline eased, just as a car overtook, beeped its horn and pulled over. Initially, I thought it was the girls, but as we approached, the doors opened and Daphne stepped out.

She was holding something in her hand and said, 'Oh, lads, I'm glad to have found you.' She held up a striped towel and said, 'The girls departed a while ago and I found this after they had left. I think it belongs to one of you three.'

We dismounted, and Nick walked over to claim his towel. After handing it over, her hands spread wide and she asked, 'Well, now that I'm here, who knows what this bonny place is called?'

I shook my head and followed her gaze. Since leaving Moffat we had steadily increased height and were now on the top of an escarpment. I had been guilty of riding with my eyes pointed towards the road and hadn't taken the time to appreciate the panoramic surroundings. Her eyes were cast to a nearby ridgeline, which plunged sharply to create a deep valley. The surrounding hills had similar fault lines, creating a massive hollow, shaped like a bathtub. From our vantage point, we couldn't see the bottom of the valley, but without prompting, were given a brief history lesson.

The four hills surrounding the hollow all had names: Great Hill, Peat Knowe, Annanhead Hill and Ericstane Hill. Together they formed a dramatic hollow called the Devil's Beef Tub, the name derived from the actions of a local clan called the Johnstones. During the 17th century, the clan carried out daring raids across the border into England, and their intrepid exploits led them to be known as The Devils.

They would lead stolen cattle into the 500-foot hollow and hide until they were safe from capture. Those seeking the cattle would also face the mist, another natural obstacle, which would roll up from the valley, clinging to the steep sides as it filled the chasm. Few men would have had the courage to enter such a place, especially knowing The Devil's notorious reputation.

It is said that the name Devil's Beef Tub may also refer to the valley's resemblance to a contemporary tub used for preserving meat. Sir Walter Scott, in his novel, *Redgauntlet*, described the Devils Beef Tub "as if four hills were laying their heads together, to shut out daylight from the dark hollow space between them. A damned deep, black, blackguard-looking abyss of a hole it is."

On this clear day, we had been oblivious to the natural crater, although we were only a few hundred yards away. I could imagine why pursuers would have problems finding such a location, especially during inclement weather when mist, rain, sleet and snow would hamper searches. Add to that, the fact that the Johnstone Clan were prepared to battle to keep their stolen beef. Mad Scotsmen in kilts, shouting battle cries as they race towards you with weapons drawn, is something I have only seen in *Braveheart* and that was scary enough!

With our historical lesson over, Daphne said, 'I hope you enjoyed that wee tale, but you'd better hurry as I'm sure you'll not want to miss the Fringe.'

As she walked towards her car, Nick called out, 'The what?'

For a few seconds we thought that she had not heard, but as she completed a U-turn and turned the car towards Moffat, she drove alongside us and replied, 'The Fringe is short for the International Fringe Festival. They have acts from across the world. That's why we thought you were heading to Edinburgh. The city will be heaving, so we guessed you'd already booked a room. Mind you, there is always the hostels if you fall short, and you're always welcome in Moffat.' Then she tooted her horn, waved, and left us alone alongside the Devil's Beef Tub.

'There goes our pub lunch,' Nick whispered and set off at speed towards Edinburgh in the hope of locating a vacant bed.

The Fringe Festival was something that we hadn't considered, but it wasn't mentioned again during the remainder of the day's ride. Silently, we blitzed through villages, hurtled down steep sections (Alan and Nick raced each other and I followed tentatively), and refused to walk up any hills. When at last farmland gave way to the outer suburbs, our pace had reduced to that of a carthorse. Nick's reddened face cried out for water, Alan's chirpy grin was yet to develop, and I was once again questioning the reasoning behind travelling so far, so quickly (for me anyway).

When a *Welcome to Edinburgh* sign came into view, Alan perked up and dashed from the rear. As he passed me, the smile returned, but neither Nick nor I had the will, speed or stamina to catch him. Despite our haste, a late departure from Moffat meant that we were now riding alongside rush hour traffic. Commuters watched through windscreens as we weaved in and out of standstill traffic and followed signs for the city.

We passed chip shops, kebab shops, betting shops and discount shops. We overtook static buses, waved to old ladies, and whizzed past old people's homes. We circumnavigated numerous roundabouts, jumped a red light, and located an array of pubs. But we found no accommodation.

There must be some kind of invisible line where discount shops end and paid accommodation takes over. We eventually located this border, just after the tenth mini roundabout.

The first establishment was full, and so was the one next door. What had we expected? We were not even remotely near the epicentre, and every other building had been converted into a place of residence for visitors. It suddenly dawned on me how popular Edinburgh was and how unprepared we were. We were riding into the city during the peak weekend of summer and expected to find a vacant room for the night. And eventually, after many more intersections, we did.

The large house was constructed from oversized, chocolate-coloured bricks, which created a gothic ambience compared to the traditional terraced houses alongside. A metal gate led us into a cottage garden towards a stout door decorated with a brass bell, which Nick rang enthusiastically. After a few seconds, a woman opened the door. She was about sixty years of age, with short grey hair and schoolteacher glasses, and she wore a knitted cardigan that draped to her knees. For a fleeting moment, there was nothing but silence as she stared at the three men in front of her. We were waiting for a rebuke. Something along the lines of, 'Ock, I'm sorry, but we dinne do all male parties.'

But instead, she smiled warmly and said, 'Goodness me. I've only this minute turned the sign from "No Vacancies" to "Vacancies". I had a cancellation, you see.'

My heart leapt and we grinned appreciatively, waiting for the door to be flung open in a homely gesture for weary travellers. But instead, she asked, 'Is it just the three of you?'

Oh no. The rebuke was coming. I could feel it, and my stomach flipped in anticipation. I couldn't go any further. Not today. Where were the girls when we needed them? Nick removed his baseball cap, stepped forward and explained, 'Yes, it's just us three at the moment. I'm meeting my wife at John O'Groats in about five days, and today we've cycled from Moffat.'

With this information, the door opened further and she replied, 'Are you those end-to-enders who cycle from Land's End to John O'Groats? How exciting. I've had a few stay here over the years. Why are you standing out there? Come inside, away from the chill. You all look tired.'

We stepped into the hallway and instantly felt at home. The walls were decorated with framed maps of faraway places, and most of the wooden floor was hidden by a woven mat that was decorated with Inca characters climbing snow-clad mountains.

'Are you cycling for a charity?' she enquired.

'Yes, for Macmillan Nurses and the Arthritis Society,' I explained eagerly.

She looked at me quizzically and replied, 'Seems like an odd pairing, but we all have our reasons.'

From her purse she pulled out a donation and waved away the thanks by saying, 'I love to travel and always donate to charities when I can.' As we stowed the notes she explained, 'I enjoy this time of year, as we get guests from across the world. A man from Buenos Aires stayed last week. He was fascinating and taught my husband to tango. She turned to me and asked, 'So where are you from, my dear?'

'Luton, just north of London,' I replied proudly.

She patted my arm and said, 'Well, my wee hen, someone has

to be, and I've heard it has a nice airport. Now then, I need to stop nattering. Let's get your key so you can freshen up for the Fringe.'

As Nick picked up his panniers, he explained that all he wanted was a meal, a beer and a bed. She listened intently as he relived the day on the road, and after showing us to our room, she exclaimed, 'Oh, it's such a shame that you're a wee bit tired. I'll tell you what. I'll make a pot of tea and you can try my homemade fruitcake after you've all had a shower.'

Nick dropped onto the nearest bed, and as she left the room, opened his mouth to speak. I chuckled and said, 'Yes, Nick, that's why you don't do hostels.'

He lay back on the bed and called out, 'I'm serious though. All I want tonight is lager, steak and sleep. I've been cycling all day, smell like a pig pen and don't need to be entertained by impoverished students trying to break into the big time.'

Alan was pulling out a new shirt from his panniers, and as it slid seamlessly into view.

I asked, 'What about you?'

He hung the shirt on a hanger, turned towards me and said with a grin, 'You know me, I'll try anything once, but first I need a wash!'

Despite the late hour, the sun still threatened to burst through the broody skyline as we made our way to the city centre in a taxi. On first impressions, our driver looked to have hailed from India. His head was adorned with an ivory-coloured turban, and his skin was a golden brown. But as soon as we sped off, his accent turned out to be as local as the famous shortbread. He chatted freely and asked lots of questions about our ride before switching the conversation to cricket, the weather, and the long winter to come.

Due to Scotland's geographical position in the northern hemisphere, summer days are gloriously long. I glanced at the car's digital clock and noted that, although it was nearly 9pm, the streetlamps were still turned off. It was hard to comprehend that in sixteen weeks this same location would go from sixteen hours of daylight to only eight. But for now I was in the moment, something that Nick, who had decided to come after all, was struggling with. The driver dropped us in the heart of the city, then wished us well as we stepped alongside throngs of people in search of a good night.

The streets were filled with hundreds of visitors. Maybe even thousands. It was hard to tell, and from the bemused look on Nick's face, I could tell he was not interested in joining them. As we stood quietly, I thought back to the previous day and the stark contrast to the sedate but pleasant streets of Moffat, just 24 hours earlier.

A lone bagpipe player stood on a street corner, adorned in a tartan kilt. The shrill sound from his instrument resonated across the streets towards the imposing turrets of Edinburgh Castle, which dominated the skyline.

We should have been primed for a night of fun and excitement, but the day's ride had taken its toll. Instead of embracing the atmosphere, we sought solace in the nearest pub. During the short walk, we were subjected to a barrage of offers by hordes of touts, eager to give away as many flyers as possible in order to claim their reward.

The streets were awash with a sea of discarded advertisements, depicting bold claims about the shows on offer. I knelt down to pick up a flyer, and while standing, had another one thrust towards me by a passing tout. Alan and Nick took an alternative approach and walked without eye contact.

By the time we found a free table, Nick was fading. Alan went in search of a pick me up and returned with a pint of lager, two local ales, and three nips of whisky. While I studied the flyer and contemplated getting them to watch something described as "an award winning spectacle combining opera, poetry and dance," Nick quietly sipped his drinks and mumbled about food. Alan took note of his request and returned with another round of drinks plus three packets of salt and vinegar crisps.

I dropped the flyer onto the table, and while devouring the crisps, contemplated my next move. I sensed anarchy if I asked them to trail the streets with me, so I finished my drink, stated the infamous words, 'I am just going outside and might be some time,' then stepped onto the busy streets.

During my melee, I encountered a spaceman, a gorilla, a buxom blonde and lots of spotty teenagers, eager to hand out glossy advertisements. I kept walking, refusing eye contact in an attempt to reduce the bombardment. A young woman stepped away from the wall, her eyes wide, and thrust a card into the gap between my shirt buttons. I smiled, walked on, then read the advert and dropped it onto the pavement. From what I knew of Nick, particularly in this state, a Russian poet riding a unicorn would not go down well.

A bearded man glided past on a skateboard. He was wearing headphones and hummed to himself as he traversed the streets, pulling flyers from a side pocket and dishing them out to anyone that looked his way.

At a street corner, I stopped at a dustbin and counted the amount of pamphlets I had been handed. I added fifteen pieces of paper to an over-flowing bin and stepped back into the crowd. One man caught my eye. He was not an astronaut, or a Martian, and he used no props. His functional clothes consisted of High Street brands, although his dark hair was unkempt and partially hid his green eyes.

He winked, stepped away from the shadows and asked how many tickets I was after. Without even thinking about the show he was promoting, I answered three. Magically, he pulled three tickets from his pocket and exclaimed, 'Well, you're a lucky man then. These are the last tickets for the hottest show in town. The last three! Honest to god. The bloke on stage will be massive, I tell you. Massive! He's on next door at ten tonight. You'll laugh your nuts off. Guaranteed. And mark my words, this time next year he'll be a headline act.'

Nick knew I would return with tickets and chuckled wearily as I explained that I'd picked up the final three tickets for this year's sensation.

'You're a nice bloke, but sometimes you're extremely gullible!' was all he could muster as we made our way to the gig.

As Nick predicted, it was not a sellout, but those that ushered alongside us were bustling with anticipation. Most seats were filled, and I felt that my impromptu choice had been a good one, despite the fact that the room resembled a scout hut rather than a theatre. We grabbed a beer each, found our seats, then waited for the lights to fade.

The show was short lived and involved a short, bald man telling jokes from various prompts on the stage. Halfway through one of the sketches, Alan leaned close and whispered, 'I've seen this bloke on TV. I'm sure of it. George Doors!'

'George who?'

'George Doors,' he whispered once more.

I had never heard of the man, but decided he might be worthy of more attention and sat upright in anticipation of further merriment. The spectators were enthusiastic and laughed far more than we did. Maybe they knew something we didn't. The difference, I suspected, was that they hadn't cycled hundreds of miles from Land's End to get here.

As the laughter increased, it was clear that the bald man had a hold on the crowd. My eyes were drooping, but I forced myself to tune into his wit. To my right, Alan stared ahead, expressionless. To my left, Nick's head drooped forward, and in between bouts of laughter from the row in front, I could hear his rhythmic snores.

As the comedian completed his brief, but appreciative set, the crowd clapped loudly and the front row called for an encore. The bald man never returned, and as the audience began to disperse, we prodded Nick and guided him to the exit.

As we walked outside, he asked, 'Did I miss anything?'

'I read the ticket a final time and explained, 'You slept through a comedy sketch by a bloke called Matt Lucas. I doubt you'll hear his name again.'

The fresh air invigorated Nick, and with a sense of purpose, he strode along the pavement and called out, 'Well, lads, now it's your turn to follow me.'

We crossed the road, walked into a Mexican restaurant and ordered flaming fajitas, washed down with ice-cold bottles of beer. As we ate, I pulled an unread advert from my pocket, describing an exhibition about David Livingstone and his Victorian encounter with Africa. Nick read the leaflet, then replied, 'Sounds great, but I'm stuffed and need a lie in.' Alan also craved downtime. It was clear we were washed out, but I was keen to get some type of cultural experience during the bike ride, and in the morning, I tiptoed out of our room in search of a bus.

16

Day 10: Riders on the Storm

"I will go anywhere, provided it is forward."
—David Livingstone

Edinburgh to Pitlochry (70 miles)

Africa has always fascinated me, and the exhibition helped fuel my appetite for returning there again one day. The walls and displays were decorated with wooden carvings from ancient tribes, detailed illustrations of slaves waiting to be sold in Zanzibar, and excerpts from Livingstone's diaries as he delved deeper into the interior.

Livingstone was first and foremost a missionary, but also made it his life's work to abolish slavery. Although his efforts did not directly bear the fruits he desired, they did stir a huge amount of public support throughout the civilised world.

Among other impressive accolades, he also became the first European to view "Mosi-oa-Tunya" (the Smoke that Thunders). After travelling by canoe to witness the splendour of the falls, he later wrote, "The whole scene was extremely beautiful; the banks and islands dotted over the river are adorned with sylvan vegetation of great variety of colour and form. No one can imagine the beauty of the view from anything witnessed in England. It had never been seen before by European eyes, but scenes so lovely must have been gazed upon by angels in their flight." He named them Victoria Falls, after his monarch.

During his time in Africa, Livingstone lost contact with the outside world while searching for the source of the River Nile. Some thought he was dead or held captive, and others speculated that he had become lost in the wilderness. No one knew for sure, and as the story gained traction, the publisher of the New York Herald commissioned a reporter by the name of Henry Stanley to find Livingstone.

Stanley accepted the challenge, and after eight months of harsh travel, located Livingstone on the shores of Lake Tanganyika in a small village called Ujiji. It is here that Stanley said the famous words, "Doctor Livingstone, I presume."

Setting out to locate the source of great rivers is not as common as it once was; most have been discovered. But that's not to say that there is nothing left to explore. Present-day British explorer, Alastair Humphreys, has created the phrase *Microadventure,* and in basic terms, it means enjoying an adventure close to home. Although he has cycled around the world and undertaken many extreme challenges, he is more likely to be found in a bivouac on an English hillside and once circumnavigated outer London on foot, staying close to (but not on) the M25.

During the dash back to our accommodation, it struck me that we were also on some kind of expedition. We were not trying to quell slavery, or search for the source of the River Severn, but our journey was unique in its own way. Back in the bed and breakfast, I asked for a dictionary and sought out the definition. Oxford gave the answer as *"an unusual and exciting or daring experience."*

Our thirteen-day expedition was a mere blip compared to these explorers' feats of endurance, but it was still a real life adventure. I hadn't discovered a long lost tribe but had nurtured my companionship with Alan and found a new friend in Nick. I sensed that our journey would not end with a framed photo at John O'Groats. There was something more to come. I felt a surge of wanderlust and began to daydream about future adventures. Maybe one day my home would be filled with nostalgic wares, collected and bartered from bazaars, flea markets and remote destinations.

It was nearly midday when we set off. Our destination was Pitlochry, a market town on the edge of the Highlands. I studied the map and found that there was only one major road leading to Pitlochry. In such hilly conditions, there couldn't be many alternative routes. This also meant that the road would be busy with traffic, including cars, motorbikes, caravans and heavy freight vehicles.

I pushed these negative thoughts aside and settled into a steady rhythm with Alan in the lead and Nick happy to remain at the back.

The further north we rode, the harsher the weather. It was closing in on all sides, akin to the pincer movement made famous by attacking Zulus. Black clouds resembled the head and horns of a mighty bull, and we were heading straight into the midst. The traffic refused to ease and thundered past as the first bolt of lightning woke the sky. Nick's luminous yellow poncho was a guiding light as I fell to the back of the pack, stared through the gloom, and wiped raindrops from my eyes.

Once again, I was in a cocoon. Once more, we were at the mercy of passing traffic and clawed our way along the A9. If there had been a pub or a café or a bothy we might have surrendered and took refuge. But we saw nothing, just driving rain shrouding the surrounding wilderness.

Unlike before, when my poncho behaved like an untamed beast, I now had it under control. It was pulled tight, and through a small gap in the hood, Nick's poncho never wavered from my sight. It was about survival. The A9 would end. There would be a room, a shower, a chance to eat, and the promise of local refreshments. It was just a matter of being patient, cranking the pedals and never, ever giving up. Dangerously, I drifted into a moronic state of neutrality and began to daydream.

Once this bike ride was over, I would contemplate a global adventure. Maybe there were still lost tribes in the Amazonian jungle to be found. I began to chuckle out loud as a thought hit me. Imagine if I became lost while in the steamy interior and a reporter from England was sent to find me. By that time, I would have located an alternative source of the Amazon River, and as the reporter approached, they would say, 'Alistair McGuinness, I presume.'

Beeeep! The sudden noise forced my eyes wide open as oversized tyres from an articulated lorry came within a foot of my head, sucking the bike into its rain-splattered slipstream. As the vehicle ploughed onwards, I fought for control, knowing that the road was too slippery for sharp movements. I was suddenly in the middle of the road and daren't risk twisting my head to look behind, but gradually I managed to ease the bike closer to the edge of the road.

I yanked the poncho hood down and wiped water from my eyes, but the constant barrage from sideways rain gave little respite. My eyes continually blinked, subconsciously attempting to flush away the water, but my vision was still impaired. The sensible option was to give up cycling and walk along the verge, but I ploughed forward at a slow pace, hoping for an imminent improvement.

From out of the gloom, Nick's yellow poncho appeared once more. They had pulled into a layby, and for the first time on the trip, I noticed a flicker of anxiety on their matted faces. Above the roar of the passing traffic and lashing rain, Alan called out, 'Nick's found another road just ahead. We need to get off. This isn't funny anymore.'

I nodded mutely and wondered what part of the afternoon had

ever been funny. I was also secretly happy. For once, they were just as worried as me about the sanity of riding in such conditions. In hindsight, we should have dropped the machismo earlier and thought about the risks. The A9 was way too dangerous, and it was with a sense of relief that Nick found the detour.

As it turned out, we had already done the hard yards and were nearer to our destination than we had thought. The storm front had passed, leaving behind a perfect rainbow, its vibrant arc ending at the base of a solitary tree, surrounded by a sea of heather. I reached into my front bag and rummaged around in search of a camera. Instead, I pulled out two granite rocks and threw them into the adjacent field. It seemed that Nick had found the Land's End memorabilia and was getting his own back at last.

Pitlochry is the gateway to the Highlands, and its population of 2,500 swells to over 5,000 in the summer months as visitors flock to the area to experience a plethora of activities including fishing, walking, bird-watching, and the most common activities of all — sightseeing and coffee shops.

Queen Victoria's doctor once recommended the fresh air in Pitlochry to those suffering ill health, and during our day's cycle ride, we had certainly inhaled plenty of the stuff. Ironically, I felt breathless and lethargic as we trundled silently past the welcome signpost. As we cycled wearily along the tree-lined high street, it was hard to imagine that this was once a frontier town. The first purpose-built road in the highlands headed directly to Pitlochry in an attempt to civilise the clans living in the wilds further north.

Cafés, guesthouses and eateries now dominate the main thoroughfare, and we noticed many were in demand as we cycled past their steamed up windows. With considerable ease, we found ourselves a bed for the night and climbed the steps to our room in silent gratitude. For once, Alan didn't sing in the shower, and my legs were reluctant to move again after a short rest on the single bed. Hunger forced us into town, but the sound of live music drifting from a nearby pub hastened our speed. As we stepped inside the warm interior, the singer struck a final chord on his guitar and announced to the cheering crowd, 'Thanks very much. Good night!'

The adjacent table was surrounded by a boisterous group of revellers, drinking and sharing stories. I sat close by and attempted to tune into their conversations. I heard snippets about travel, mosquito bites, budget accommodation and must-see attractions.

Most of the group were less than thirty years of age, and from their accents, I guessed they were a mixed crowd of international visitors. While heading back from the toilet, I veered towards their table and managed to make eye contact with one of the girls while she was in mid-sentence. She was olive-skinned and wiry with long dark hair, and she spoke with a Mediterranean accent. I guessed she was Spanish and returned her gaze with a smile. With a newfound confidence, I sat alongside her for an impromptu chat and discovered that she was a Gap Year student from Brazil.

As I had guessed, they were mostly strangers to the town and also to each other, thrown together for one night by a chance meeting at the local youth hostel. Some were in the area for the sole purpose of climbing the highest mountain in Scotland, Ben Nevis. Others were in search of the Loch Ness Monster, and a few were sheltering from the bad weather before resuming a walking tour of the Highlands. They looked to be a healthy bunch, and conversations flowed seamlessly in multiple languages.

I wanted to call Alan and Nick over, so that they could witness and experience the positive effects of staying in youth hostels. But when I glanced over, they were sitting by the fireside, happily content and sharing stories. I left the girl and joined them. The gentle warmth from the low flames, together with the demanding day and late night beers, sapped my strength. I announced an early departure, leaving them in mid-discussion, then plodded through the damp streets to my bed.

Nick and Alan

17

Day 11: Three miles high

"There are two seasons in Scotland. June and winter."
—Billy Connolly

Pitlochry to Aviemore (58 miles)

I woke early, drew back the curtains and cast my eyes to the sky. The day ahead looked bleak. If there were any high peaked mountains nearby, we would not gaze upon them today. During breakfast I asked our landlady if she knew what the forthcoming weather would be like. She was a quiet lady and had not chatted much during our overnight stay, and all she could muster was, 'No doubt there will be rain and mist, but no snow. Not for a wee while anyway.'

The thought of snow seemed ludicrous. This was our summer holiday. But our destination was Aviemore, a popular ski resort in the Highlands. It was now the final week of August. In fifteen weeks it would be Christmas, and I had once skied near Aviemore on Boxing Day.

On that occasion, I drove up with Steve (the adventure sports instructor now living in Newquay). During the eight-hour journey, the outside temperatures had crept lower and lower, and by the time we arrived in Aviemore, it was minus twelve degrees.

The following morning, we snuggled into our skiing gear, stepped into arctic conditions, and walked carefully along salted roads to the nearby chair lifts. Blizzards were forecast, and the attendant at the cable car called out that we were lucky to get on, as he was expecting to close it down any second.

As freezing snow pelted our unprotected faces, I could understand why. By the time we reached the summit, the visibility was down to thirty feet and the upper attendant shouted something about an approaching storm. Then he pointed to the nearest slope and announced we needed to ski back down immediately. But adjacent to the ski lift, a small café in the shape of an igloo offered the chance of solace, and we dived inside for a hot chocolate instead.

As we savoured the drinks, the walls of the igloo quivered, and the handful of skiers inside were caught in a quandary. Some wanted to flee. Others thought it safer to stay. The decision was made for us. The door burst open and in walked a man of the mountains. He stood nearly six-foot-tall with fresh snow clinging to every edifice.

His long beard was coated white, and after removing a pair of icy goggles he announced, 'Everyone off the mountain. Now! We're evacuating this building. Grab your skis, follow me and stick together!'

Steve jumped up first and ran to the counter. He purchased the remaining Mars Bar on sale, and as we made our way to the door, he snapped it in half and said, 'You might need this, mate, if we get lost.'

We stepped outside to search for the remaining skiers and our guide, but they had vanished in the mist. There seemed to be only one way off the mountain, so we pushed off together, but within seconds, we had lost each other. Skiing in whiteouts is not fun. You ski blindly into the unknown.

I survived the downhill mystery tour, skiing into bright sunshine and stopping alongside a black run. I devoured the fractured Mars Bar while waiting for Steve to appear from the fog.

Now, I was returning to Aviemore, but the zest I felt many years earlier had vanished. I was lethargic, unmotivated and unhappy. I had hit the wall. The A9 had sapped my strength, and it was with a sense of foreboding that I crammed clothes into my panniers and joined Alan and Nick by the roadside.

Mist clung to the roadside, shrouding the mountains, and permeated through damp layers into my bones. I was in no mood to make small talk and felt content to remain at the back. The others seemed to be in a similar mood, and with quiet discipline we set off, changed into a low gear, and ventured forward. Time and surroundings meant nothing. There was just myself, two riders directly ahead, my tightly bound poncho, and the road under my wheels. Passing traffic became a bearable irritant, and like a tortured man accustomed to beatings, I no longer flinched as articulated lorries brushed dangerously close.

A village appeared from the gloom, causing passing traffic to slow, and the respite tempted Nick to veer onto the pavement. We dismounted, agreed on refreshments, and went in search of a café. As my hands clasped a piping hot mug of tea, I overheard Alan talking with the owner. The village we were in was called Dalwhinnie, and by all accounts was the highest in the Highlands.

Maybe it was the tea, or the bacon sandwich, or the fact that we had unwittingly ticked off a unique location, but we left the café in chirpier spirits then we had arrived. Perhaps it was my imagination, but the grey surroundings were lighter. The sun was there, somewhere. Just waiting to burst through and warm our backs.

As we set off, I overtook Nick and took the lead. He smiled and made a joke about yellow jerseys. Two mugs of tea slushed in my stomach, and I reached out to grab a Mars Bar from my bag. Riding no-handed, I cracked it into two, devoured my half and thought about another friend, half a world away in Newquay.

Aviemore was a welcome sight, and as we pedalled into town in the late afternoon, tiny gaps began to appear in the low clouds, giving fleeting views of the nearby hills. By the time we found a room, showered and stepped back onto the street, the clouds had retreated. The town was eerily quiet. Maybe all the walkers had gotten lost in the mist. The reason, I sensed, was less adventurous. It was a Tuesday evening near the end of the holiday season. Most visitors would now be tucked up in wooden cabins or enjoying dessert at a welcoming restaurant.

We walked stiffly through the streets, chose the first pub that sold hot food, and devoured the Aberdeen Angus steaks set down before us. As we ate, Alan nursed his knee, Nick complained about back twinges, and I grumbled about shooting pains in my legs. Alan sensed that we were ready to abandon the night and convinced us to try out another venue to lift our spirits.

A sports bar offered the chance for a game of pool, and we found ourselves competing with a bunch of local lads. They were reserved at first, when challenged to a game, but as the balls rolled along the green velvet, conversations opened up. Work was the focal topic. Some were unemployed, others worked in the timber industry, and one or two were seasonal mountain guides, waiting for snow.

Each of them held a pint of beer; a few also had whisky glasses on the table, which they sipped casually between gulps of lager. After returning with another round of drinks, they asked what we did for work. Nick took the initiative, explaining the technicalities of fixing machines while production managers paced the corridors and constantly asked for progress reports.

The conversation then changed to bike riding. Some of them enjoyed mountain bike rides in the local forests, but none of them could see the attraction of our long distance attempt.

One man, the tallest of the group with limp black hair and a goofy grin, rammed the black ball home and said, 'None of ye can hardly walk, let alone cycle.' He pointed to me and said, 'Look at the wee fellow, his legs are seized, and you two look like you need to be in bed.'

'Oh, it's only early yet,' Alan replied quickly and then added, 'and we only have to cycle 80 miles tomorrow.'

The lanky man downed his beer and stepped closer. I sensed that the conversation could rapidly steer off course and frantically searched for common ground. All I could think of were Dad's escapades on the pitch at Wembley two decades earlier. They stared at me with skeptical eyes as I relived his antics, and the lanky guy snarled, 'So your dad's Scottish and once nicked a piece of Wembley stadium, but you sound like a cockney. Sounds a bit strange to me.'

The whole day had been strange. He was way off the mark with my accent, but I wasn't in the mood for confrontation, and deep down I sensed that they weren't either. Tomorrow we would be gone. In a few months the snow would return, and I hoped the season would be beneficial for them and the town.

We departed with handshakes and the promise to send a postcard, which caused a few chuckles as we made our way to a table by the fireside. It was unlit, but tall stacks of split logs had been carefully placed into recesses either side of the grate. Winter was coming.

I took another look at the sports bar. Giant TV screens were placed evenly around the room, bolted firmly onto the brick walls, in readiness for the skiers and snowboarders who would trundle in after a day on the mountainside. But, for now, they displayed highlights of a recent football match, and the few patrons remaining in the bar were absorbed by a game.

I was in no mood for TV or any more games of pool. Alan appeared with three glasses, swilling with fifteen-year-old whisky from the Dalwhinnie distillery. I knocked my drink back in one go, forgoing all etiquette. Wood-smoke and honey caught in my throat, and as I stood to leave, I grasped Alan's shoulder. It had been a long day. I placed the glass on the table, mumbled a farewell, waved to the pool players and went off to collapse in yet another bed.

18

Day 12: Don't Pay the Ferryman

"The best laid schemes o' mice an' men, Gang aft agley, [*often go astray*]."
—Robert Burns

Aviemore to Golspie (81 miles)

The early night had reinvigorated me. I was the first to shower, ate breakfast alone, and finished packing as they woke. They had lingered in the pub far longer than I had envisaged and gingerly came to life while I made them tea. Their clothes had been soaked in a midnight downpour, and I watched as they wrapped them in plastic before stowing them in their panniers.

During breakfast, I checked the map, consulted with the waitress, and was informed that the village of Dornach would suffice as a likely destination to lay our heads. The others agreed, and as we departed once more, it suddenly struck me that this was our last full day on the road. Despite the lingering dampness and drifting mist, we bounded down the steps towards our bikes and chatted incessantly about how quickly it was all coming to an end.

Tomorrow we were destined to reach John O'Groats, and if we planned our day, could be there by early afternoon. I didn't want to think of the future. Only the now. I felt compelled to try a stint at the front, and as I passed Nick, he handed me a batch of Trivial Pursuit cards. Between passing cars, dual carriageways, hills up and hills down, we managed to answer a multitude of questions. At times they took ages to complete, as traffic and wind tore away our words.

It went something like this:

Three astride: 'Right you two, in which...'

'Car coming!'

Single file.

'All clear.'

Three astride: 'In which country would you find the…'

'Lorry approaching.'

Single file.

Three astride: 'Where is the highest railway in Europe?'

'What did you say?'

'The highest railway? Where is it?'

'In the world?'

'No, in Europe.'

'Sorry. Couldn't hear for the wind.'

'Highest railway you say?'

'Yes.'

'That's easy. It's…'

'Downhill section approaching.'

'Switzelaaaaaaaand.'

When we tired of Trivial Pursuit, our gaze became naturally drawn to the right-hand-side of the road. An explosion of purple heather dominated the landscape, its creases and contours resembling a giant flying carpet. Trees were rare, and those we saw were stunted and lonely. The land beyond was untamed. Once a place where wolves roamed, it is still home to golden eagles, ospreys, wildcats, deer and badgers.

Cairngorms National Park is twice the size of the Lake District and covers six per cent of Scotland. From the A9, the distant peaks looked dark and rounded, but from experience, I knew they were not easy accomplishments.

The Scottish Highlands may not be the highest range in Europe, but winter snowstorms have claimed many lives on the hills and peaks. From afar, the peaks looked inviting. Up close and personal, I knew the granite chasms and sheer rock faces could be deadly.

My time at the front ended abruptly. It was nearing lunchtime and I reached into my pack for an apple, momentarily taking my eye off the road. While riding one handed, my wheel struck something soft, bouncing me off my seat. In that blurred instant, I saw a fluffy creature under my wheel. I dropped the apple as the wheel bumped over the animal and involuntarily came to an abrupt stop when the rear wheels locked. My eyes were instinctively drawn to the chain and rear sprocket, where the eyes of a dead, wild hare stared back at me.

I jumped off the bike and moved alongside, aghast at the carnage.

I put my hands on my head, unable to pull the hare from the chain, and found myself hopping involuntarily by the side of the road.

Alan pulled over to investigate and removed the carcass lodged between the pedals and the chain. As he did so, he called out, 'You can stop doing the Highland fling. It's been dead about a week.'

Ashamed at my squeamishness, I relegated myself to the rear as we set our sights on the Moray Firth. This triangular inlet of the North Sea carves deep into the upper east coast, and we were approaching its southern-most point. The Moray Firth ends at Duncansby Head, just a few miles from John O'Groats.

Signs for Inverness appeared, but we ignored the urge to take the left turnings, instead circumnavigating the city and setting our sights on the Kessock Bridge, spanning 787 feet across the Beauly Firth. Designed by a German engineer by the name of Hellmut Homberg, the cable-stayed bridge was an inspiring sight. A brisk wind met us head on. We rode onto the imposing structure and found ourselves high above the navigable waterway, where container ships and trawlers churned through the oily waters.

Upon our descent to land, I estimated that we were now in the upper third of Scotland, and with each mile away from Inverness, the landscape grew harsher. Cities were no longer required, towns shrunk in size, and some villages were nothing more than a smattering of houses.

On the far side, we found a café, perched on high ground with spectacular views of the peninsular. A series of low-lying hills dominated the skyline; their curvaceous sides were the colour of burnt hazel. Below the hills, fertile land dotted with farms cascaded down to the water's edge.

Inside the café, promotional posters displayed articles on dolphin-watching activities, with newspaper clippings of past sightings, and advertisements for boat trips on the water. While our fish and chips were being cooked, I read the articles and discovered that the Moray Firth was home to the only known resident population of bottlenose dolphins in the North Sea.

It was hard to think of the stretch of water surrounding us as the North Sea. Such a place conjured up images of wild winds, isolated oil platforms, and fishing trawlers crashing through giant waves. The open sea was close by, a few miles east, and the next landfall would be Norway, hundreds of miles away.

The café was also home to a detailed wall map of the area, depicting roads, inlets, places of interest and accommodation. As we studied the diagram, Nick noticed a dotted line across the water and enquired at the counter.

While passing our food over, the waitress explained, 'That's the ferry from Cromarty to Nigg. It's very popular in the summer, but mainly with locals or those off the beaten track. Most visitors are in too much of a hurry these days and do the inlet route by road. Do you want ketchup? Its 20 pence extra.'

The road to Cromarty, situated on the tip of the Black Isle, was glorious. It looped from the café, wound along the headland, and dropped sedately to the foreshore. The Black Isle is not an island but a peninsula, dotted with farms and blessed with hidden coves, marshland, and a series of small cliffs. The fertile waters are also home to colonies of seals, and according to the articles on the café wall, the local fishermen co-exist alongside the wildlife.

Here was a place I could revisit. Just like the Wye Valley, it was a location that I never knew existed before our bike ride. In many ways it reminded me of the west coast of Ireland, with its earthy aromas, rugged headland, and sense of community. People waved from gardens, dogs barked from behind gateways, and birds swooped low in search of insects. It was as though the area had its own unique microclimate. A day earlier, we were fighting fatigue and hypothermia. Further north, and we were basking in late summer sunshine.

According to the signpost, the village of Cromarty is twinned with Brigadoon. I had always thought Brigadoon to be a mythical Scottish village, hidden in the mist. Cromarty itself had a mystical appeal, with its petite harbour and panoramic views of the Moray Firth, which lapped against the base of distant hills.

We followed signposts for the ferry and found ourselves on a small quayside. Built in the 18th century, the working harbour is in constant use by local fishermen, but the ferry only runs for part of the year, due to inclement weather and a lack of visitors in the depths of winter.

We cycled off the quayside, along a slip ramp, and found ourselves at the end of the road. King James IV regularly crossed these waters as part of his pilgrimages to the shrine of St. Duthac at Tain in the late 1400s. The mediaeval craft that would have transported him safely to the other side of the wide inlet would have been in sharp contrast to the boat that was now bobbing towards us.

While sunning ourselves by the side of the road, a car stopped alongside, and I took a peek to see the passengers. Excited children peered through open windows as they awaited the ferry's arrival. I felt proud of their parents for taking the time to experience an alternative route. Maybe I was wrong and they lived close by, and this was their normal commuter route. But the children's smiles, as the ferry approached, told me this was a rare treat.

I turned to study the boat. My initial thought was that it resembled a miniature troop carrier, similar to those used in Normandy during the D-Day landings. The bow of the ship was not designed for speed, but functionality. Instead of a streamlined design, the upper part of the bow was, in fact, a metal ramp, wide enough for one car. As the ferry stopped, it was lowered by chain onto the slip road, revealing the main deck and its cargo.

The cargo consisted of one car, one person on foot, and two cyclists. The car exited first, beeping its horn with a gesture of thanks, followed by the cyclists, who smiled as they freewheeled past, changed gear and headed inland. The single passenger walked tentatively down the ramp, using a cane to steady himself, and as we cycled towards the ramp, he touched his flat cap and wished us good day.

Just before departure, another car appeared from the hills, and the captain directed it onto the ferry, alongside the first. There was no room for any more. As a child I had enjoyed ferry trips to Ireland and marvelled at the array of decks inside the massive hulls. Thousands of cars packed into a tin container as it churned through the Irish Sea.

During these trips, there was little chance of meeting the captain, but on our little craft, I was able to stand alongside him as he navigated the familiar passage with assured confidence. The water was black but glistened in the sunshine, and more than once, we caught the sight of fins churning through the water as dolphins swam close by.

It felt good to be moving without pedalling, and for a short while, we stood silently by the metal railings, each of us lost in thought as the boat chugged through deep water, skirted a wooded headland, and set course for the village of Nigg.

As the boat approached land, the captain pulled a switch, and the cars began to turn around. They had been parked on a round metal plate, which now turned 180 degrees so that they could drive off in a forward direction. As the ramp lowered, we thanked him, waved to the children and then cycled off the boat. Just before changing gear, I stole a final look at the ferry and noted the name displayed on the hull. It was called the Cromarty Rose.

Nigg looked just as appealing as Cromarty, but the steep road leading down to its slipway meant we had little time to appreciate the stone cottages and farmyards. Once more we were silent until we plateaued and took the time to look back at our path. Far below, the

Cromarty Rose was returning to its home, carving through the dark waters and leaving a creamy trail in its wake.

The sun was to our left, dropping towards the distant mountains. The air was cooler now, catching at my throat as I filled my lungs. The skyline was dominated by a series of elongated clouds, smeared across the horizon as if by the lazy stroke of an artist's palette knife. The sun was catching them now, blushing their pale sides as nightfall drew closer.

It would be a magical sunset across the peninsula, but not one that we would ever see. We had to keep moving, and with a chirpy reluctance, we cast our eyes from the headland and set them towards the village of Dornoch.

Despite the many hours spent riding, a nagging doubt kept racing through my mind. Tomorrow was the last day, and I didn't want it to be an epic battle. I was hoping that we would arrive at our final destination within a reasonable time, feeling elated and not fatigued. The weather had been kind, and I felt that we needed to take further advantage of the conditions. In Scotland, two days of similar weather are rare.

I kept my thoughts to myself as we resumed the game of racing to village signposts, and as the sun dropped lower, the miles tumbled. It was only as we rode into Dornoch did I make my feelings known. The Tourist Information Centre was about to close for the evening, but the woman behind the counter seemed delighted to help the last minute customers.

Just before Nick enquired about accommodation, I calmly explained, 'Sorry, lads, but I think we need to keep moving. Tomorrow is a big day, and I don't want to be worn-out at the end.'

She looked at me, then at the others and asked, 'Are you cycling to John O'Groats?' We nodded in agreement and she replied, 'Well, my opinion, for what is it worth, is to keep going if you can. If you encounter a northerly wind tomorrow, you'll have a tough day.'

She studied us for a split second and said, 'Though I must admit, you all look a bit weather-beaten.'

It was the first time I had really studied our complexion, and where she saw tiredness, I saw a healthy ruggedness. The sun had touched our faces, and our arms were the colour of burnt copper. Had I ever been fitter? Maybe so, but it had been a long time since I had felt so contented. I just needed to get a few miles nearer to our final destination before nightfall, but also appreciated that my companions were ready for hot food and refreshments before bed.

Alan replied first and said, 'Well, I'm happy to keep moving. A few more miles won't hurt, and you can get the first round of beers in.'

Nick nodded in agreement, and with the help of the assistant, we booked into a bed and breakfast 15 miles further north, in a village called Golspie.

As we departed, she called out, 'Go swiftly, lads, as it will be dark soon enough. At least now you'll have plenty of energy left for the Berriedale Braes.'

By the open door, Alan asked, 'What are they?'

She chuckled softly and replied, 'Oh, just a few wee hills to remind you that you're in bonny Scotland.'

We followed her advice and raced against the sun. During that final hour of daylight, we rode under a blazing sky as the veil of cirrostratus clouds that had been forming overhead burst into colour. The road cut inland for a spell through a tapestry of farmland and pine plantations. Despite the fading light, the North Sea could still be glimpsed in places, far to our right.

Lights began to appear, as farmhouses hidden among the low lying hills prepared for nightfall. The road dipped towards an inlet, and we crossed another bridge up ahead on the left, a blackened mound loomed ominously, its summit shrouded in mist. At its base, we passed a signpost, and in the fading light, I noted the distance remaining. In four miles we would arrive in Golspie.

That would leave 72 miles to complete our journey. All we needed to do on the final day was navigate a final hurdle — the Berriedale Braes. Silence descended during the last few miles, and the frantic pace was replaced by a monotonous grind. We entered the village, subconsciously made our way to the main street, and located our accommodation with miraculous ease.

A few hours earlier, I had picked up a pamphlet about Golspie while at the Tourist Information Centre, and by all accounts, it was a charming seaside town with a long sandy beach and small harbour, home to a flotilla of family run fishing boats. Wherever the beach was, it would forever remain a secret. A long list of historical houses also sounded appealing, but not as enticing as a meal and a comfortable bed.

I showered first, raced to the nearest pub to order food before the chef's departure, and as we devoured dinner, I thanked the lads for giving me 15 more miles. Smiles had returned and weary legs forgotten as we ventured around the village on our final pub-crawl. Our bravado was short lived. After 80 miles in the saddle, yawns came easily. In the final pub, Alan returned from the bar with three glasses of whisky, and we raised our glasses one last time.

As we made our way home, Alan said, 'Well, lads, that was a top day, and tomorrow I fancy racing down the Berriedale Braes. Who's up for the challenge?'

Within twenty minutes we were all tucked up in bed. I lay awake, listening to every sound. Their breathing was deep and relaxed and nothing would wake them. An open window offered the chance of fresh air, and I kneeled on my bed to peer outside. A gap in the clouds gave a rare glimpse of distant stars, their bright pinpricks surrounded by blackness. Somewhere nearby an owl tooted. We were so close to the end now.

Down in the courtyard, the wind stirred, and I was convinced I could hear the creaking of rope as a boat tugged at its moorings. I felt the salty air in my throat, and I breathed it in deeply. Sleep was imminent; I could no longer fight it.

Boarding the Cromarty Rose

19

Day 13: Champagne Supernova

"Now this is not the end. It is not even the beginning of the end. But it is, perhaps, the end of the beginning."
—**Winston Churchill**

Golspie to John O'Groats (81 miles)

After showering, I pulled on my last pair of fresh underpants and looked outside the bedroom window. Nick was below, kneeling on the cobblestones with his bike upside down as he made final adjustments. I opened the window further and called out his name.

'Morning,' he said. 'Just changing a few broken spokes and giving the bikes a final check over.'

As I closed the window, I thought back to the last twelve days. How many times had he repaired broken spokes? It seemed part of the daily ritual, the same as Alan popping painkillers and rubbing Deep Heat into his knee every morning.

By the time I arrived in the courtyard, Nick had finished with his bike and was now fiddling with the Donegal Flyer. He looked up, smiled, and then said, 'Just checking your brakes for the Berriedale Braes.'

I had forgotten all about the infamous inclines, and as breakfast was being served, their name surfaced once more. The landlady overheard our conversation, and as she placed down more toast, explained, 'Oh, don't be worrying about them wee hills. Not today anyway. You look like a healthy bunch, and from the snoring last night, you're well rested. Just mind the hairpin bend at the bottom and be sure to check your brakes before you need them!'

She topped up our teapot and added, 'Now, if you were going to cycle down them in mid-winter or in driving rain, then I would say you were half mad. Those hills can be dangerous, so don't do anything silly this close to John O'Groats. Now then, you'd better be off. You'll want to get to the signpost before it closes.'

'How can a signpost be closed?' I asked.

'Oh, the man that owns it takes it away each evening, so it doesn't get pinched!'

With her words of advice ringing in our ears, we strapped the panniers onto the bikes for the final time and set off in glorious sunshine. In places, the single road to John O'Groats was only a few hundred yards from the North Sea, running parallel with the shoreline.

The terrain was dominated by farmland, occasionally fragmented by sections of pine forests, their sharp lines and obtuse angles clashing with the natural contours of the nearby ridges. In parts, all that remained of the plantations were multiple rows of sawn off trunks, protruding from mud stained hillsides.

Nick pinged a spoke and we pulled over for a stop. A few miles later, he lost another. Each pit stop absorbed time, and although we were tantalisingly close to our destination, the relaxed start meant we were in danger of arriving too late for a photo by the signpost.

The village of Helmsdale appeared, nestled between the sea and a surrounding hill known as Bun-Ullidh, its blanket of gorse emblazoned in purple. To enter the town, you cross Helmsdale River and have the choice of two bridges. One is old and the other is new. The A9 is aligned with the new bridge, which is built near to what is left of Helmsdale Castle. All that remains of this ancient fort is a plaque and a coffee shop. As we dashed across the Helmsdale River, we were blessed with a fleeting glimpse of the original bridge in its entire splendour. Built in 1811 by Thomas Telford, its two granite arches, each 70 feet wide, form the backbone under which the wide river flows into the sea.

I turned my head to look in the opposite direction and was rewarded with a panoramic view of the harbour. It looked to be a place of solitude, but where there were now just a few boats, in 1818 the scene would have been very different. The North Sea is a natural spawning ground for herring, and their numbers were once so prolific that millions were trawled without a strategy in place to sustain the industry.

During the mid 19th century, the community flourished as the demand from Europe for oily fish increased. At its peak, 700 women were employed to gut, clean, wash and salt the fish, and an army of coopers were employed to construct wooden barrels in which to house the fish during their export to Europe.

With little control on quotas, fish stocks plummeted, and by the end of the First World War, the boom was over. Population declined, and the village is now home to only a thousand people. Today, the small selection of boats found at the harbour target prawns and lobsters, as well as herring. Fishermen adhere to strict EU guidelines that take into consideration off limit seasons (due to spawning) and sustainable quotas.

Out of the thousand people that reside in Helmsdale, we sighted just two — a middle-aged couple walking their dog. They waved as we cycled by, and within a few minutes, we were out of town, changing gear once more as the next incline appeared.

What goes up must go down, and with each uphill revolution, I sensed that the Berriedale Braes were nearby. I knew that the hairpin bend was close to sea level, and from where we were, the dark water looked to be far below to our right. The road levelled, and in the distance I could see a signpost. Alan and Nick surged forward, unable to hide their enthusiasm. As they passed the Berriedale Braes sign, they turned briefly to wave to me.

Like a pair of puppies unleashed, they attacked the downhill incline with vigour. I was determined to follow and pushed hard to keep them in my sights, but with each bend they pulled away. The road angled further, and I subconsciously reached for the brakes as a series of curves rapidly approached. For a split second, my heart missed a beat as I failed to lean accordingly and over steered towards the white line. But if I didn't let myself go now, when would I ever get the chance again? As the next corner appeared, I found my racing line and tucked my head in low, ignoring the urge to tap the brakes. I needed to feel the wind in my face, and as dense foliage blurred past, I thought of nothing except gripping the handlebars. Suddenly I was free, and all the miles, pain, doubt and daydreaming had been worth it.

The free-fall was short lived. The Donegal Flyer was never designed for such speeds, and with the overstuffed panniers, I could feel the rear wheel bouncing as I leaned into the next corner. I pushed away negative thoughts, allowed the bike to flow around the bend, and suddenly I was approaching sea level.

For a fleeting second, I was on a bridge and caught sight of a feisty stream tumbling towards sea. The land on the other side of the bridge was the complete inverse of the downhill section, and the momentum I had gained quickly dissipated. Within seconds I was crawling along in the lowest gear. This was the final hurdle between me and John O'Groats, but the angle of the sun told me that the day was far from young. Somewhere, many miles away, a man would be waiting for visitors to have a photo taken by his end-to-end signpost. Please let him still be there, I heard myself whisper as I dug deep and attacked the hill.

I didn't see Alan and Nick until I reached the top. Cars passed by, their inhabitants glancing over to catch my grimace. One or two honked horns as a welcome gesture, but I didn't look up. I couldn't. All I could do was think of the summit and a man with a rented signpost. We were so close, yet nothing would make me walk.

Unlike the secret hill near Cheddar that left us fighting for breath, the difference in our fitness was spectacular. As I approached the top, I could feel my heart pounding, but felt exhilarated rather than exhausted. The lads were staring out to sea, and I turned to face their gaze. Far below, nestled between the cliffs and the river mouth was a row of whitewashed cottages. How wonderful, I thought, to rest for a while on one of their doorsteps with a steaming cup of tea, watching the river tumble into the sea.

But that would have to wait for another day. We were ready to continue, and for the next hour, I rode on Nick's tail as Alan set a blistering pace. My slipstreaming skills had improved vastly, and as we moved steadily along the road, my eyes flickered between Nick's rear wheel and the dark sea just to our right. On the horizon I could just make out the silhouette of a fishing trawler. When I scanned the water again, it had vanished.

The ambient light was playing tricks on me. Now I was convinced I could hear music. Was I hallucinating? Breakfast had been a rushed affair, as we had been keen for a swift departure and had eaten very little since. Maybe my blood sugar was low. But no, there it was again. It was bagpipes. But where was it coming from? The road ahead was devoid of traffic, people and houses. Maybe a kilted Scotsman was on a nearby hillside, busking to weary end-to-enders. I looked around and saw no hills, just undulating tundra falling towards the sea.

As the music grew louder, I recognised the tune. It was Amazing Grace. The lyrics flooded my thoughts and I found myself humming the words, "*I once was lost but now am found. Was blind, but now I see.*"

Alan and Nick slowed and then turned their heads to look behind just as a car crept past, each window wide open. From inside, beaming smiles from Karen and Sam as the wailing sound of bagpipes played from their car speakers. They stopped by the side of the road, and we embraced in a group hug. While we had been cycling, they too had sought out adventures and there were many tales to tell.

But first, there was unfinished business to attend to. The girls took our panniers and set off to John O'Groats to search for accommodation and a man with a signpost. With the panniers now gone, the difference was liberating. The Donegal Flyer was unleashed, and without the bulging weight, it zipped easily along the windswept road.

The route meandered inland towards an area devoid of hills. This far north I had expected craggy summits, but I was met instead by miles and miles of level paddocks, dissected neatly by stone walls, and inhabited by hundreds of sheep.

Wick was another surprise. I was expecting a small town clinging to the edge of a rugged coastline. What I discovered was a town large enough to house 7,000 people, built around a wide river, which flowed sedately through its busy centre. It was strange to see hustle and bustle after so many miles of isolation. There were Indian takeaways, cafés, betting shops, banks, manicured parks and numerous roundabouts. Most houses were constructed from dark stone, each rectangle block surrounded by a line of mortar, so that they resembled Lego play sets.

We settled for a (very) late lunch of Mars Bars washed down with Lucozade, and didn't linger long enough to appreciate the town. Nick calculated that we were still about fifteen miles from John O'Groats, and the hours were racing by. With no panniers and a sugar high, the remainder of the ride was a breeze. Not even a blanket of light cloud could dampen our spirits as we hurtled along the A99 at speed.

A car approached from the opposite direction, loaded down with bikes. As it flashed past, I thought I saw someone waving and was proven correct a few moments later. It completed a U-turn and drove alongside, just as a girl with wild, frizzy hair popped her head out from the passenger window.

'What took you so long?' she called out loudly, and then added, 'Well done, lads. We left you a message in the visitor's book at the hotel.' They completed another U-turn, and with a flurry of waves and beeps of the car horn, they were gone.

During the next hour, the road drifted close to the shoreline and then weaved further inland, cutting us off from a sea view. Occasionally, we discovered abandoned farmhouses, their slate roofs collapsed, exposing ancient timber trusses, now fractured and splintered by the elements. Most farmhouses were smaller than the ones we had previously encountered, and some along the A99 were in need of attention. Mildew clung to roofs, and whitewashed exteriors looked grubby and pitted.

Not all buildings were in need of repair. Many houses were in fine condition, decorated with hanging baskets, and in some we noticed children's climbing frames, or tiny goal posts positioned carefully on freshly mown front lawns.

The surrounding land was a mixture of wild heather, long grass, and bog. In places it had been cultivated, but away from the farms, it looked wild and untouched. We were very close now. There were no more roads to turn down. No further chance of taking an incorrect turn, and no more opportunities to ask locals which way to go.

The sea was no longer visible to our right, temporarily hidden by a wide ridge of mottled grass. But it was clearly noticeable straight ahead — a darker shade of grey than the blanket of clouds that shrouded the peninsula. If the sea was this close, it meant only one thing. We were nearing the end of the road. After thirteen days, our eyes were conditioned to spotting signposts for new villages, towns and cities. We had raced to many during this period and knew that the words written on the white sign ahead would confirm that we had arrived in John O'Groats.

This time, there was no frantic dash. In fact, we eased our pace, subconsciously trying to stretch out the moment for as long as possible. When the time came, we rode three abreast with arms held high. There was no one around to share our glory. It was just a small, white signpost, three tired bikes, a grey sky threatening rain, and us.

A surge of adrenalin rushed through me as we cycled onward towards the sea. Up ahead was a post office, and I thought back to Ron the postmaster at Land's End. How many end-to-enders had he registered since our departure 13 days earlier, I wondered. Where were they all now? Some might be hurtling across the Severn Bridge; others might be huddled in a bothy near Shap. I quietly smiled at the thought that one or two may have discovered Nick's secret hill.

A mum and toddler emerged from a shop and we waved. They stopped by the doorway and returned our greeting. Suddenly the village disappeared, replaced by farmland once more. I could smell the sea and greedily inhaled the salty air. Houses appeared, some of them displaying bed and breakfast signs by their front gates.

We overtook a parked car, its passengers lost in thought as they studied a road map, and up ahead the road turned for one final time, leading us into a large oval-shaped car park. There was life here. Visitors were everywhere. Some carried daypacks on their backs, and others sat outside a café, watching the world go by. A minivan, filled with tourists, vacated the car park just as we arrived.

We threaded around cars as they contemplated which free spot to choose and cycled past a boarded up shop advertising an assortment of delicious ice creams. As we passed the Tourist Information Centre, a family emerged, grasping maps, flyers and memorabilia. One of the children was about ten years of age, and he waved as we skirted the building in search of the girls and the end-to-end signpost.

They were up ahead, calling our names, waving and smiling. We rode onto a grassy embankment overlooking the sea, and while dismounting, a bottle of champagne appeared, wrapped in a packet of frozen peas. During hugs, kisses, handshakes and woops of joy, the cork was popped. It launched into the overcast sky where the wind snatched it away towards the rocks.

Plastic flutes were filled and toasts made, as we huddled together and stared out to sea. Across the water, a few miles away, I could see a pocket of low-lying land. It was the Isle of Stroma, once a home for hundreds of people, but over time, the hardships of carving an existence in such a wild and isolated environment led to an exodus. The last families abandoned their homes in the 1960s.

There was a feeling of being at the edge of the world, but in reality, Scotland exists for many more miles north. Out of sight, were two more sets of islands, known as Shetland and Orkney, and within this archipelago, you will find 26 inhabited islands. Villages on the most northerly islands are nearer to the Arctic Circle than they are to London. Ferries are their lifelines, and while Sam refilled the flutes, we watched as a boat left the adjacent harbour, bound for a faraway isle.

For the passengers on board, their journey was just beginning, but ours was nearly over. We had two more tasks to complete. The girls had convinced the signpost man to remain open, and he stood nearby, waiting for his well-earned fee.

Twenty years later, I still have the photo. I now live in Australia and it takes pride of place in my house. Whenever I study the image, I think back to that eventful day. We were dizzy with happiness, fighting fit and bursting with confidence. The final task was to write our names in the official logbook, which was located in the John O'Groats Hotel, a few yards away.

The hotel was an imposing whitewashed building that dominated the headland and had uninterrupted views of the sea. The main entrance was two stories high, with a gothic spire perched high above an octagon structure.

While leaning my bike on the outside wall, I noticed that the exterior was losing its battle with the elements. The whitewashed cladding was cracked and had turned a blemished pale of grey. The interior also looked tired and run down, but the staff were endearing, and as soon as we entered, they handed over the official logbook. It was nothing fancy; just a hardback A4 book, filled with comments and illustrations from successful end-to-enders.

The previous entry in the logbook was from the foursome, and true to their word, they had written a short snippet about beating the three cyclists from down south. For a few moments, we contemplated a witty reply, but somehow it just seemed too hard. We settled for a simple entry, with just our names, the date and a few sentences. No witty poem from Alan, no enlightened words from Nick. It had been a long day, and the panoramic views from the hotel bar were too spectacular to ignore any longer.

We ordered drinks, settled by the conservatory window, and shared stories. Outside, a squally downpour sent walkers fleeing for cover. Before leaving, Alan purchased a postcard from the front desk, scribbled a few witty lines and posted it to Jim, the Talking Beard, c/o the Coronation Pub, Southport.

I stole a few minutes alone and ventured outside, catching a moment of sunshine between showers. A wooden bench created a perfect resting place for me to gather my thoughts. As I gazed upon the windswept peninsula, the reality of achieving our goal finally hit me. I clenched my fist in acknowledgement and greeted a passing walker with a ridiculously wide grin. Was it the endorphins triggering such positive vibes? Maybe it was. But there was something more.

While accomplishing the ride, I had managed to confront and deal with the feelings of despair that had clouded me since Mum had died. For the first time since wearing a batman mask and cloak as a child, I felt invincible. I was glad that the girls had been involved in our trip, and I could sense that something special was happening between Alan and Sam. I heard my name being called and turned to face the hotel. My friends were calling, and it was time to depart.

By sunset we had showered and went in search of a secret spot recommended by a volunteer from the Tourist Information Centre. It was definitely secretive, as it took the taxi driver numerous attempts along lonely roads to find our destination for dinner — the Fisherman's Retreat.

It was a ramshackle building, filled with faded photos of fishing boats, family portraits and village life, from long, long ago. It seemed poignant to be in the fisherman's house while his wife prepared the catch of the day. He was a man of few words with a shock of grey hair, a vice like grip, and a face that had weathered many storms.

His voice had a soothing brogue, and while leading us into his lounge, he explained, 'Make yourselves at home. I'll be in the back room if you need anything.' Before he departed, we spotted a record player and asked if it was OK to use.

'Aye, of course. Play 'til you're tired,' he said, and closed the door gently, leaving us alone in his lounge. His wife was a spirited soul, less than five feet tall and eager to please as she prepared the tables. As she handed out menus, she found us studying the vinyl record collection and exclaimed, 'Good luck with finding anything other than Val Doonican,' and before we could reply, she silently returned to the kitchen.

'Val Doonican it is,' I said, while the girls prepared drinks.

The lounge led through to a decking area surrounded by transparent plastic sheets, which bellowed softly from the onshore wind. Our table was soon adorned with bowls of food. The seasonal vegetables were steamed to perfection, and the boiled potatoes had split perfectly, like flowers in bloom. Their mottled skins flaked easily as we scooped them from the steaming pot with earnest. A sizzling pan of freshly caught herring, still intact with heads and tails, was placed alongside a rack of warm bread, and every morsel was devoured.

As we ate, the girls shared tales about their time in Scotland, and we did the same. In between sips of wine, the dessert menu appeared along with a complimentary wee dram from the fisherman's wife. As the evening drew to an end, Nick and Karen moved closer in whispered conversation.

Eventually, the music stopped, and for a short while we listened to the rising wind as it tapped softly against the plastic surrounds. I was eager to hear one more song and left the table to rake through the collection of vinyl memorabilia. The fisherman's wife had been correct. Apart from records that should only be played at Christmas or New Year, the choice was limited.

I chose an LP, placed it on the turntable, and watched as the automatic arm moved towards the first track. As the crackling chords permeated through the rooms, I sank into a leather chair, took a sip of whisky, embracing the essence of wood smoke and honey as it warmed my throat.

My head was giddy and my eyes felt heavy, but I finished the drink and set the empty glass onto the floor. As I did so, my eyes caught sight of Alan and Sam. They were in silhouette by the table, the flicker of a single candle illuminating the small distance between them.

I smiled, then closed my eyes a final time and thought back to a windswept beach in Blackpool eight weeks earlier, as Val Doonican sang;

> *Don't be concerned, it will not harm you*
> *It's only me pursuing something I'm not sure of*
> *Across my dreams with nets of wonder*
> *I chase the bright elusive butterfly of love*
> The End.

In memory of Alice McNelis and Christine Godfrey.

Alan, Ali and Nick at John O'Groats.

20

John O'Groats

In 2010, John O'Groats was named the winner of the Carbuncle Award. This is the kind of award a location that manages to attract over 100,000 visitors a year does *not* want to win; the only prestige that comes with winning is being recognised as the "most dismal town in Scotland."

The awards were created by a magazine called Urban Realm, who specialise in architecture and design, and are passionate about how Scotland's towns and buildings look and feel. Not everyone agrees with their opinions, and they lead to heated debate each year. However, naming and shaming seems to work, and the award wasn't all bad news for John O'Groats.

In recent years, a consortium has been assembled to reinvigorate the town, and the effects have been positive. The community now has a motto: *Experience the Wilds.*

The hotel closed down shortly after we visited, and was at one time in danger of being demolished. But it has since been stylishly reincarnated and renamed as The Inn at John O'Groats.

No longer do visitors complete a U-turn within minutes of arrival at John O'Groats. In summer months, they are offered sea safaris and guided walks. If they want to browse, craft shops selling local wares are available, and the cafés sell freshly ground coffee and traditional food.

Even so, unfortunately not everyone was a winner of the changes. The man that took his signpost home each evening, and held the rights to take the photos by the end-to-end icon, became a victim of the revamp. A new sign was cemented into the ground at the original site and is now a free attraction!

21

Gretna

Cupid's arrow fell upon Alan and Sam in Gretna Green, and after a whirlwind romance, they were married. A few years later, they moved to Western Australia with their son, Blake, to live by the Indian Ocean. They decided that their new life under the sun would not be complete without a dog and soon fell in love with a jet black groodle. They named their puppy Gretna, in memory of a special day, a long time ago.

Gretna is bouncy, mischievous and fun. While in Australia, she loved jumping in their family pool and swimming in the nearby ocean. Nowadays, she can likely be found being walked in the ancient woods close to Ampthill, as they eventually returned to the UK and now live close to Karen and Nick.

They enjoy cooking together and music is part of their lives. Alan and Nick still cycle regularly and can often be spotted trail-blazing across the Bedfordshire hills at sunset, on route to their local pub after many miles in the saddle.

Gretna

22

Later

A year after the bike ride, Alan's mum, Christine, passed away after her brave battle with cancer. In the same year, I climbed to the top of Mount Blanc, the highest peak in Western Europe, with Steve. At the summit, we shared a Mars Bar and watched the sun rise over the Alps.

Soon after, I commenced circuit-training classes, and halfway through a sprint across the floor, bumped into a girl. Her name was Francine, and during a drink in the bar, I discovered that she was funny, feisty, and compassionate. She also had a yearning for adventure. Later that year, she travelled with Dad and me to the Isle of Skye. Within two years we were married.

In 2003, I was made redundant after thirteen years with General Motors, and we decided to leave England to embark on a global adventure across South America and Africa. Ten weeks after the factory gates closed, we were working as conservation volunteers in the Amazon jungle, contemplating a permanent move to Australia.

Our story was published in 2015.

It is called: *Half a World Away: Jungle Guides, African Tribes and a Donkey called Angus.*

23

Authors Note

I hope you enjoyed *End to End: John O'Groats, Broken Spokes and a Dog called Gretna* and wish you good luck if you are contemplating a similar adventure. If you have a few moments to spare, I would really appreciate an online review.

Happy travels,
Alistair

I enjoy keeping in touch with readers. You can find me at the following locations:

Web @ alistairmcguinness.com
Facebook @ Half A World Away
Twitter @ amcguinness1

24

Acknowledgments

Without the positive support and encouraging words from my wife, Francine, and our two children, Noah and Sebastian, the story would never have been told. I owe them many hugs!

I am also indebted to my parents and siblings.
Mum raised us to be respectful and taught me to laugh at the smallest things.
Dad inspired me to travel and challenged me to learn.
Alice Marie made me tea and toast, just when I needed it most.
Andy taught me that life-changing surprises are always possible.
Dave encouraged me to explore, taught me to navigate and lent me his bike.
Matthew taught me to dance and never gave up on me.
Michael introduced me to music and taught me the power of self-belief.

Thanks to Packard Images for designing the amazing retro style cover.
Alan Godfrey and Jenny Warr added the lively illustrations, and I admire their talents.

Alan and Nick deserve particular attention. Without their camaraderie, humour and adventurous streak, our journey would never have been worth sharing!

Special praise goes to all those that care for cancer sufferers.
During the ride, we raised £1500 pounds for Macmillan Nurses.

CPSIA information can be obtained
at www.ICGtesting.com
Printed in the USA
BVHW042248151218
535717BV00020B/682/P

9 780994 316509